D0861361

R. BUCKMINSTER FULLER

The Kassler Lectures

Other books in the series:
<u>Toyo Ito: Forces of Nature</u>, Jessie Turnbull, ed.

Publication is made possible in part by a grant
from the Barr Ferree Foundation Fund, Department
of Art and Archaeology, Princeton University.

R. BUCKMINSTER FULLER

WORLD MAN

DANIEL LÓPEZ-PÉREZ, EDITOR
WITH CONTRIBUTIONS BY ALEJANDRO ZAERA-POLO AND STAN ALLEN

PRINCETON UNIVERSITY
SCHOOL OF ARCHITECTURE

AND

PRINCETON ARCHITECTURAL PRESS
NEW YORK

CONTENTS

PREFACE

This volume is the second in a series of books based on the Kassler Lectures, held at the Princeton University School of Architecture. It documents the series' inaugural address, delivered in 1966 by R. Buckminster Fuller (1895–1983). Kenneth Stone Kassler (1905–64), in whose memory the lecture series was founded, attended the school and served as an instructor and design critic here for more than three decades. An admirer of Fuller, whose research into new building materials and technologies resonated with his own, Kassler was responsible for bringing the renowned inventor and author to Princeton for a series of visits throughout the 1950s and 1960s. During his extended presence on campus, Fuller acted as an animating force, lecturing, teaching seminars and studios, and engaging students in groundbreaking structural and cartographic experiments.

The publication of Fuller's lecture today is timely. The text testifies to a period when the School of Architecture was invested in the exploration of new technologies and counted among its ranks figures who best represented architecture's active involvement with science. The convergence of Fuller and other design scientists such as Victor and Aladar Olgyay (widely considered the fathers of environmental architecture) at Princeton in the mid-twentieth century gave rise to a culture of technology that has since nearly disappeared and needs to be reinvigorated. For a brief time, Princeton functioned as a laboratory and broadcasting device for important technological and structural advances in architecture.

Fuller's reliance on collective experimentation at the school traces a model of education committed to capturing the innovations of the moment rather than reinforcing long-standing academic traditions, styles, or pedagogy.

That educational model, based on the agility and flexibility needed to rapidly confront urgent social or environmental issues, seems particularly appropriate today as a strategy to exploit the size and qualities of the Princeton School of Architecture.

Fuller's profile is one of breathtaking currency. The indefatigable polemicist and educator had a difficult relationship with architecture. Lacking formal training, he constantly remained on the edge of the profession, never fully accepted by his fellow architects; nor was he embraced by the scientific community, which looked down on him as someone without the requisite credentials or disciplinary rigor. A follower of the gay science tradition, Fuller was forced to defend his role as a public intellectual who tinkered with architecture and engineering, ecology and economy in order to transform them all.

The public, in fact, was much more appreciative of Fuller's ideas than any of the professionals whose fields he intersected. Possibly the best-known architectural figure of his era, Fuller had a tremendous capacity to ignite public interest in his projects and their causes. This capacity marks his career as a precursor of what professional practice has now become, with architects needing to interact with a growing list of stakeholders and public interfaces throughout the process of making a building.

Other aspects of Fuller's 1966 lecture at Princeton similarly forecast critical issues facing architecture today. The lecture's title, "World Man," not only alludes to the speaker's "world citizenship" (Fuller famously wore two watches—one set to his office's time and the other set to the local time of whatever country he found himself in) but also clearly acknowledges that many of the problems architects faced at the time were global in nature. Fuller's lecture of a half-century ago anticipated what is now common knowledge: that local actions have universal consequences. Architecture, for Fuller, required a global scope of vision.

Fuller addresses ecology and the environment in his lecture, having already identified these as crucial subjects for architecture. His references to energy, fossil fuels, food, and pollution describe the modern world as an ecosystem to be reconciled with nature. Again, we need to remind ourselves that it was 1966, before the first oil crisis and the emergence of broad ecological consciousness. Coincidentally, this lecture took place the same year Complexity and Contradiction in Architecture was published.

In his talk, Fuller also anticipates our present knowledge-based economy. He refers constantly to economic processes, as if capitalist development could actually become an integral part of natural ecosystems and political frameworks. For Fuller, patents were an essential part of the new knowledge economy; the architect/scientist was less an artist or technician than an entrepreneur who redefines the regimes of power surrounding practice in order to retrieve agency from the more conventional modes of patronage. This entrepreneurial orientation foreshadows the various forms of archi-tectural agency that we are experiencing now, which similarly defy the tradi-tional relations between architects and clients. Through these approaches, the discipline becomes truly political.

Fuller's understanding of the political engagement of architecture and technology is genuinely prophetic. At a time when the *cosmopolitical* has become a common subject of discussion across the sciences and humanities, Fuller's global, eco-systemic, entrepreneurial, and political view of architectural practice perfectly embodies the contemporary notion that a politics not attached to the cosmos is moot and that a cosmos detached from politics is irrelevant. This book, the crystallization of an event that occurred several decades ago at Princeton, can be read as a visionary moment in the history of the discipline. And isn't that capacity to be visionary and experimental, to capture and forecast the emerging, the true task of a school of architecture?

I would like to thank Stan Allen, my predecessor as dean, for initiating, in association with Princeton Architectural Press, the series of books that document the Kassler Lectures, and for mobilizing the infrastructure to make this particular volume happen. I would also like to extend my thanks to Daniel López-Pérez for his thorough analysis of the lecture and his work in producing the book; to Daniel Claro for his discovery of Fuller's manuscript in the Archive of the School of Architecture; to former dean Robert Geddes for his important contribution to the book; to the Barr Ferree Foundation Publication Fund at Princeton University, which generously supported this publication; to the College of Arts and Sciences at the University of San Diego, which kindly provided funds to the project's editor through a Faculty Research Grant; to John Ferry of the R. Buckminster Fuller Estate and to Chuck Hoberman for their help with obtaining images; to Nancy Eklund Later for her editorial contribution; and to Alice Chung for her inventive book design.

—Alejandro Zaera-Polo

BEAR ISLAND
SUNSET
POST OFFICE
MAINE

*copies sent
to Mrs. Kessler
&
Mr. Jordl
8/30*

*Oct 12 - Wed George
Oct 5 - Wed   Oct 5-*

August 26ᵗʰ 1966 –

Dear Dr Geddes –

Your letter of July 20ᵗʰ has
been forwarded to me from my office.
I am indeed honoured and deeply moved
to be invited to give the first Kessler
Memorial Lecture in my dear friend's
memory. A day, during the first
two weeks of October would be
possible for me to come to Princeton.
Should such a time be satisfactory to you

will you let me know which day? I expect to return to my office September 16th. We could discuss it by telephone — when I have my complete schedule before me — if earlier on later would be better.

I am also willing to have the lecture published. I speak entirely extemporaneously without notes, so the address should be taped & transcribed & corrected from the tapes. The reception should be a delightful opportunity to see old friends — and new.

Faithfully yours

Buckminster Fuller

Letter to Robert Geddes, dean of the Princeton School of Architecture, handwritten by Anne Hewlett Fuller and signed by R. Buckminster Fuller, Bear Island, Maine, 26 August 1966

INTRODUCTION

DANIEL LÓPEZ-PÉREZ

On August 26, 1966, Richard Buckminster Fuller wrote to Robert Geddes, accepting the invitation of the recently appointed dean of the Princeton University School of Architecture and Urban Planning to deliver the inaugural Kenneth Stone Kassler Memorial Lecture. In a handwritten letter dictated to his wife, Anne Hewlett Fuller, and signed by him, Fuller cautioned Geddes that he would "speak entirely extemporaneously, without notes." A month or so later, on October 5, Fuller addressed an audience of architecture students, faculty, and area practitioners in a process of "thinking out loud cumulatively," as had become "the pattern for [his] life." Speaking on themes he had been rehearsing in his mind for decades, Fuller delivered one of his most compelling assessments of the struggles facing man in the mid-twentieth century.[1]

Fuller opened his lecture by telling of how he had recently been asked by a national magazine to imagine being appointed Building Commissioner of the United States. The editors were interested to know what he, if given the power, would do to solve the nation's significant urban problems. Fuller quickly dismissed the very idea as enforcing one's will upon others—an ineffectual way of approaching these problems, he maintained, given the natural checks and balances of evolution. Looking beyond the post of U.S. commissioner, or "building czar" of the "political state," Fuller mused on grander aspirations: "Why not…make me world

czar of building," or better yet, "czar of building the Universe?"

The problem this posed, Fuller conceded, was that that position was already filled. "I am deeply impressed," he confessed, "with the designer of the universe; I am confident I couldn't have done anywhere near such a good job." Instead, Fuller made his mission the *study* of the universe and of its "extraordinary design." It was in the space between national "czar of building" and "czar of building the Universe"—between influencing a nation and changing the world— that Fuller envisioned his role. His was a search to understand man's place in the world and the world's place in the universe. He pursued this, in his Kassler address as in his long and productive career, by starting with the questions: What is man doing in the Universe? What is he supposed to be doing? What does he think he is doing?

When Fuller arrived at Princeton to deliver his lecture, the seventy-one-year-old was already a well-known figure in contemporary architecture and design. In January 1964, he had been profiled in Time magazine. The inventor of "houses that fly and bathrooms without water… cars and maps and ways of living bearing the mysterious word 'Dymaxion,'" Fuller was "best known" at the time, the editors asserted, for his "massive mid-century breakthrough known as the 'geodesic dome.'"[2] His early work on industrialized housing and his studies of structural

PRINCETON
ALUMNI WEEKLY

Vol LIV · NOVEMBER 27, 1953 · No. 10

Tensegrity Sphere, built on the Princeton University campus by Fuller and
students, featured in the 27 November 1953 edition of the Princeton Alumni
Weekly. The cover caption reads, "With the help of the fire department
apparatus, graduate students put the final touches on an architectural
experiment which has excited nationwide attention."

geometry had culminated in the 1950s in his development of the geodesic dome and his articulation of the geodesic and tensegrity principles that underpinned it. Designed to provide maximum volumetric enclosure and environmental control using a minimum of means, Fuller's invention found a ready audience during the postwar period and quickly proliferated around the globe.[3] In 1966 he was at work on his geodesic tour de force—the United States Pavilion for the World's Fair—which would open a year later in Montreal at Expo '67.

If Fuller's domes brought him great public notoriety, they also earned him a place in the pantheon of modern architecture. In the mid-1950s, a scale model of one of his geodesic domes joined the collection of the Museum of Modern Art (MoMA) in New York, and in 1960 his two-mile hemispherical Dome over Midtown Manhattan featured prominently in the museum's <u>Visionary Architecture</u> exhibition.[4] Fuller's reputation as a technological visionary had been confirmed a year earlier, when Arthur Drexler, director of the Department of Architecture and Design, installed three of his "mathematical structures" in MoMA's outdoor sculpture garden.[5] Alongside bronzes by Gaston Lachaise and Aristide Maillol, Drexler exhibited a geodesic dome, tensegrity mast, and space frame, in an effort to add "new grist to the modern architectural discourse." The exhibition succeeded in drawing thousands of visitors to what trustees of the museum later acknowledged was "essentially a show of structural engineering."[6] A photograph of the structures, illuminated at night in the museum's courtyard, has become ubiquitous in Fuller's monographs.

Fuller never trained as an architect, but his influence on contemporary architecture—although in no way normative—was beyond dispute the year he lectured at Princeton. Seventeen of his most significant patents related to structural and cartographic innovations had already been granted, and a vast number of articles documenting his inventions had appeared in the architectural press. In 1962 a monograph devoted to his work, edited by John McHale, was published as part of George Braziller's popular Makers of Contemporary Architecture series. As McHale explained elsewhere around that time, "Any discussion of the impact of technology on architecture… must, inevitably, involve due consideration of the unique contribution of Buckminster Fuller."[7]

Fuller's notoriety may have come from inventing a number of revolutionary artifacts, but his "unique contribution" in the professional sphere came from the concepts, or operative principles, he explored through those works— concepts that had the power to alter man's relationship to the world. "In 1927," Fuller explained, "I made a bargain with myself that I'd discover the principles operative in the universe and turn them over to my fellow men."[8] Fuller spent much of the 1950s and 1960s circling the globe, hosting workshops and lecturing on these principles; a charismatic and infatigable speaker, he arguably asserted greater influence with his words than with his inventions.[9] But the common thread of Fuller's output was these operating principles: "He [saw] himself quite simply," Time observed, "as a kind of technological avatar, come for the liberation of mankind."

As Geddes explained when introducing Fuller to the Princeton audience, the mission of the Kassler Lectures was to bring to the university distinguished speakers from the "field of environmental design," which he defined as "the field of architecture, engineering, industrial design, city planning and its related arts." Fuller was an ideal inaugural speaker, given that his research cut across these disciplines, which had previously been considered distinct areas of study. Geddes called Fuller "hard to classify… either [an] engineer or architect or inventor or discoverer or geographer or mathematician or all of these," proof of the importance the dean attributed to the cross-disciplinary nature of Fuller's research. At the height of his professional career and public influence, the mature Fuller provided an extraordinary point of departure for the new lecture series.[10]

Fuller had brought his ideas to Princeton previously. In 1953 the "advocate of the theory of light-weight, over-all economy in building" constructed on its campus "the largest discontinuous compression sphere ever to be erected."[11] The sphere was built by students in front of the Architectural Laboratory, a center for experimentation in environmental studies and technology founded by Princeton's School of Architecture in 1949. During an impressive two-week period, Fuller and his team constructed the sphere from ninety 1½-inch aluminum struts held together by a network of $3/16$-inch steel aircraft cables. The structure enclosed 32,000 cubic feet, or enough volume to accommodate a 2,000-square-foot, eight-room, two-story dwelling. The virtue of this remarkable structure was its lightness: whereas the equivalent volume built from traditional housing materials would weigh an average of 150 tons, this sphere weighed only 650 pounds.[12]

Giving form to the sphere was Fuller's principle of "discontinuous-compression." As he would later define in his "Tensile-Integrity Structures" patent, a discontinuous-compression structure comprised a combination of compression members in the shape of "struts." Held together by cables, or "slings," these members worked in tension in such a way as to evenly distribute structural forces without any strut touching any other strut, thus producing the principle of "discontinuous-compression."[13] The essence of "Tensile-Integrity Structures" resided "in the discovery of how to progressively reduce

Tensegrity Sphere. The 40-foot sphere was built from 90 independent metal struts held together by a network of cables, which evenly distributed loads throughout the lightweight structure.

PRINCETON BUILDS LARGE GLOBE MAP

6½-Foot 'Earth' Designed to Give Architect Better Geographic Knowledge

Special to The New York Times.

PRINCETON, N. J., April 6 —A large globe map of the earth, a sphere six and a half feet in diameter, constructed of metal tubing and clear plastic, will be completed early next week at Princeton University.

The globe was designed by Dr. R. Buckminster Fuller, who designed the "Golden Dome" for the American Exhibition in Moscow last year. He built it in the university's architectural laboratory with the assistance of twelve students from the Graduate School of Architecture.

Called a geoscope, the globe will be suspended inside a glass room. It is intended to provide a better comprehension of world geography to help architects plan their work in a larger perspective, Dr. Fuller said.

He noted that ordinary globes were thrown out of proportion when they were enlarged for general use.

Dr. Fuller said the trouble with conventional globes was that they were built with latitudes and longitudes, which represent areas of the world by spherical squares. "However, you cannot put a square on a sphere," he pointed out.

The geoscope eliminates this problem by dividing the world into spherical triangles. One of the chief obstacles to its construction was that the information necessary to "triangulate" the Soviet Union was not available.

Since it is covered with transparent plastic, the geoscope is a "true planetarium," the 64-year-old scientist said. As the student watches the heavens through the clear "crust" of the device he will be able to see and feel the earth revolving in the presence of stars.

CONSTRUCTING MODEL OF EARTH: Dr. R. Buckminster Fuller discusses globe he designed with Stuart M. Hutchison, left, and J. Robert Hillier, Princeton Graduate School of Architecture students who are assisting him.

Alan W. Richards

Geoscope, constructed inside Princeton's Architectural Lab by Fuller and students, featured in the 6 April 1960 edition of the New York Times. Unambiguously modeled on planet Earth, the globe map, Fuller claimed, was four times larger than any accurate cartographic sphere in existence at the time.

the aspect of compression in a structure so that...the structure will have the aspect of continuous tension throughout and the compression will be subjugated so that the compression elements become small islands in a sea of tension."[14]

For Fuller, the general shift away from compression and toward tension aimed to "bring the slenderness, lightness and strength of the suspension bridge cable into the realm previously dominated by the compression columns concept of building."[15] His invention produced an effect "akin to taking some of the compression out of the 'compression towers,' i.e. the columns, walls, and roof, of a building through the creation of a structure having discontinuous compression and continuous tension [in which] the islands of compression in the mast are progressively reduced in individual size and total mass."[16] By reducing the overall structural mass through an assemblage of struts that do not touch and by increasing the ratio of tension over compression through the use of cables, Fuller discovered strength through lightness. As he notes in his Kassler lecture, he envisioned this architectural experiment as "point[ing] the way to practical solutions of actual building problems." Discontinuous-compression domes had the potential to revolutionize the construction industry, and they formed the basis of a number of important patents Fuller would apply for and receive.[17]

But the Princeton project demonstrated something more than structural efficiency. In an article entitled "The Sphere of Ideas," published in the Princeton Alumni Weekly, the model was described as representing nothing less than the "characteristic structural principle of the universe." It was "no accident," the article explained, "that the sphere is 40 feet in diameter. Mr. Fuller believes that the discontinuous compression principle is the characteristic structural principle of the universe. And with a 40-foot diameter, his sphere becomes a sort of scale model of the world, at 1:1,000,000."[18] For Fuller, Princeton's discontinuous-compression sphere was both a revolutionary architectural solution, unprecedented in its scale and lightness, and a conceptual model of the universe itself. As such, it served to illustrate his belief that experimentation in search of a better understanding of nature's operative principles was key to the future well-being of mankind and the universe.

In the spring of 1960, Fuller returned to Princeton to build another sphere with students, this time in the form of a geo-scope, unambiguously modeled on planet Earth. Claimed by Fuller to be four times larger than any accurate cartographic sphere in existence, the 6 ½-foot sphere was constructed of metal tubing and several layers of clear plastic film, inscribed with illustrations of the continents. It was suspended inside the large, glazed room of the Architectural Lab, a space used to research natural daylighting effects on scaled architectural models, and it was a great cartographic achievement. The Daily Princetonian hailed it as the "best globe map...ever built."[19] Fuller had identified a problem with Mercator projection, commonly used in mapping the Earth, which subdivided the planet's surface into squares by means of latitudinal and longitudinal lines. "You cannot put a square on a sphere," he insisted.[20] In his Dymaxion Map patent of 1946, Fuller presented an alternative method of charting the globe by inscribing a polyhedron within a sphere and projecting the Earth's surface on its triangular faces. This method of subdivision produced less distortion than either its square predecessor or other known cartographic systems of projection. Thus, the geoscope offered a more accurate representation of the Earth's forms and landmasses.

Fuller had built a geoscope previously, at Cornell University in 1952. Although the Cornell model was much larger, the Princeton version was more intricate and arguably more accurate.[21] At Princeton, he separated the geodesic structure from the transparent surface of the globe so that the natural geographic properties of the Earth and the conceptual lines of his geometry could be studied independently but also viewed in juxtaposition. In a volume documenting the project's construction, James Robert Hillier (a professor in the School of Architecture who was a student of Fuller at the time) describes the model's capacity to integrate multiple layers of information on its surface in order to visualize relationships between vast amounts of data as the project's greatest potential. "The system of lights on the Geoscope," Hillier observed, "would allow a visitor to locate his house on the Earth through a complex system of IBM machines." The light system similarly facilitated "plotting the location of ships on the oceans...[and] the migration of masses and raw materials." The geoscope could serve as a measuring tool for diagramming complex relationships and also projecting them in time—both backward into history and into the future:

Using the same system of lights and computers it could be possible to diagram the history of the world's weather and then, by studying the trends or simply by speeding up the computer so that it had the momentum to carry its diagram ahead by a few years, it could be possible to make general predictions on the world's future weather.[22]

In a letter discussing his geoscope projects, Fuller described them as "unexpectedly" marrying his geographical and geodesic structural explorations into a single model, a demonstration that in his mind these had become effectively one and the same.[23] The structural models represented the organizational protocols of natural form and could in

Fuller, surrounded by geodesic models in the
Architectural Lab at Princeton, about 1953

Geoscope, constructed of clear plastic inscribed
with the continents and hung from a network of
hollow metal tubing, about 1960

turn be used as measuring devices for mapping and measuring the Earth's geography.

The geoscope proved a useful tool for geographers, but Fuller's intended audience for his invention was architects. As he explained to a <u>New York Times</u> reporter, he created the project to "provide a better comprehension of world geography to help architects plan their work in a larger perspective."[24] That perspective reflected Fuller's holistic view of Earth and challenged the image of humankind as somehow independent of the environment. The clear surface of the Princeton Geoscope could be read both from outside the sphere looking in toward the center and from inside the sphere looking out at the firmament. Looking in, one could view Earth's geography more accurately than ever before, whereas looking out, one could begin to determine one's position within an ever-expanding universe. This two-way perspective underscored the basic relativity of human perception: the expanding universe was simultaneously "your private sky." By creating an instrument that contextualized the individual's relative point of view, Fuller helped the world look at itself.[25]

In his 1953 and 1960 visits to Princeton, Fuller formulated and explored cartographic and structural concepts by constructing physical models. In his 1966 Kassler lecture, he also built conceptual models, but this time with words. He engaged his audience in open dialogue, using language as a platform for representing relationships between the conceptual and the physical, the cognitive and the experiential. Deciphering the meaning of Fuller's words constitutes a collective process of "experimentation" in itself, as the correspondence between word and idea remained for Fuller the subject of continual exploration rather than exposition.[26]

Fuller structures his lecture using clear, deductive logic. He starts with a number of concepts, many of which he introduces as dualities: "brain" and "mind," the "physical" and the "metaphysical," the "entropic" and the "antientropic." From these dualities he posits a "theory of functions": functions are relational and exist "only by virtue of the always and only coexistence of other functions." He proceeds by offering generalizations of increasing complexity regarding these opposing functions. These generalizations give rise to new words whose accrued meanings are clear only within the context of Fuller's developing narrative. While "dymaxion"—a synthesis of "dynamic" and "maximum" that refers to Fuller's concept of employing technology and resources to maximum advantage with minimal expenditure of energy and material—is perhaps the most famous neologism in Fuller's idiosyncratic lexicon, countless other terms are introduced throughout his 1966 lecture and in its associated literature.[27]

In his talk, Fuller raises a number of questions about our relationship to the environment across all scales, from the personal to the cosmic. He identifies dual universes: the physical universe, which is "entropic" and "expansive, increasingly diffuse, increasingly disorderly"; and our cognitive understanding of the universe, which is "antientropic" and increasingly ordered. Within these two opposing orders, Fuller seeks a balance. In view of the continual oscillation between "physical expansion" and "metaphysical contraction" in the universe, he expresses his wonder at nature's anticipatory capacity for regeneration. In the face of what he describes as our "total envi-ronmental challenge," Fuller points to our "antientropic effectiveness" as our capacity as "prime designers" to find new forms of order and principles.

Essential to this process of balance and regeneration is an expanded notion of "wealth," one that for Fuller is not based purely on material resources but also includes social accountability. He defines this wealth as "the organized capability to deal with our forward metabolic regeneration." A feedback loop between material and social resources emerges: "[T]he more we use our real wealth, which is this organized capability, the more it improves and the more it increases." Fuller sees our chances of reaching this "organized capability for forward regeneration" as "magnificently weighted on the side of success." It is in

our capacity to translate "material" into "energy wealth" that he finds our true potential to harness the existing "energy flows of the universe" in order to "do the most with the least."

Fuller closes the lecture by focusing on social accountability. Aligning his aspirations with those of a younger generation—whose loyalty he describes as centered not on family, university, or even country but rather on the world— he makes a prophecy: "[T]he young world is about to take the initiative as inventor-scientist, and in the employing of principles which are operative in universities will succeed in converting the resources available to us to such a high order of effectiveness as to take care of 100% of humanity."[28]

Fuller's spherical models can be understood today as oscillating between concrete physical artifacts that revolu-tionized the worlds of structural design, shelter, and cartography on the one hand and dynamic representations of nature and of our relationship to the environ-ment on the other. Similarly, the terms of Fuller's lecture synthesize their literal and conceptual meanings in search of the most comprehensive knowledge of both— of man in his world. The spherical models constructed on the Princeton campus and the words and concepts developed in the Kassler lecture can be seen as material and conceptual experiments in the fluid and irreducible relationship between the physical and the metaphysical,

Princeton students building geodesic models
alongside the Tensegrity Sphere, in front of the
Architectural Lab, 1953

Geoscope, featured on the cover of the 22 April
1960 edition of the <u>Princeton Alumni Weekly</u>

ultimately transforming our understanding of both. As the lecture's title, "World Man," suggests, Fuller reimagines the relationship between ourselves and our environment, constructing a new future that continues to reshape the present.

Today scholars continue to rediscover Fuller and deepen our understanding of his legacy. For Buckminster Fuller: Starting with the Universe, the retrospective held at the Whitney Museum of American Art in New York in 2008, K. Michael Hays described Fuller's progression from the 4-D system of the 1920s to the versions of the geoscope in the 1950s and 1960s as based on the development of a "geological diagram": a "system in terms of movements, distances, patterns, and intensities…that is centered on the Earth as an environment and a planet in a cosmos."[29] Hays emphasizes that Fuller's geological diagram is not "an abstraction that transcends all possible experience," but rather "an empirical system of differential relations that creates and organizes actual times, movements, trajectories, and ultimately sensations."[30]

Hays argues that Fuller's geoscope is endowed with the "cognitive and perceptual" possibilities of "a 'macro-micro-Universe-information' machine, geo-info-video-dome for the comparative display of flows, patterns, and intensities of population, climate, geology, sociology, finance, and their distributions and interactions."[31] In this sense, the geoscope

project at Princeton was a precursor of the Geographic Information Systems so ubiquitous and foundational to our daily lives, bringing together real-time geographical information and complex data modeling, and constantly recalculating a projection of the future. Whether predicting alternative routes from live traffic patterns or deciphering future sociological and political changes in the population through census-data management and feedback, these systems mediate the relationship between the individual and the collective, between us and the environment. Similarly, Fuller's lifelong epistemological pursuit—his defining and redefining of words and concepts through a process of discursive experimentation, which reached a peak in the language of his patent applications and Synergetics Dictionary—foreshadows our contemporary understanding of innovation as transcending questions of technology to focus instead on issues of intellectual property.

Fuller's geological diagrams run counter to the contemporary disciplinary emphasis on specialization in architecture, which had already begun to emerge by the time he delivered his Kassler lecture. In his brief for the International Union of Architects' "World Design Science Decade, 1965–1975," Fuller warned about the dangers of specialization and pointed to architects as "the last species of professional comprehensivists" capable of facing the technological, environmental, and political challenges ahead.[32] His models call for a more comprehensive understanding of the contribution that the discipline can make in reshaping our environment— materially, but also socially, politically, and culturally. In "World Man"—and, by example, in all of his creative practices— Fuller urges architects to understand their role in society not only as technical specialists but also as public intellectuals, uniquely positioned to build alliances with the professional, civic, and cultural spheres in order to influence them all. If Fuller habitually defined himself as a "comprehensive anticipatory design scientist" who championed broad thinking in order to benefit the greatest number, our revisiting of his "World Man" lecture almost half a century after it was delivered challenges us to examine our disciplinary definitions as a way to seize the present and transform the future.

NOTES

1. R. Buckminster Fuller to Dr. Robert Geddes, Bear Island, Maine, 26 August 1966; and R. Buckminster Fuller, "World Man," typescript of lecture delivered on October 5, 1966. Both documents, reprinted in their entirety in this volume, are held in the Robert Geddes Papers, Princeton University School of Architecture Archive, Princeton University, Princeton, N.J. In his letter to Geddes, Fuller recommends that his lecture be "taped, transcribed, and corrected" for eventual publication. All subsequent citations of Fuller are taken from this typescript unless otherwise noted.

2. "The Dymaxion American," Time 83, no. 2 (10 January 1964): 48. The issue's cover illustration features Fuller's radome, Dymaxion car, tensegrity octahedron, 4-D apartment house, and Dymaxion mobile laboratory alongside his disembodied head, contoured in the shape of a geodesic sphere.

3. The Time article maintains that in 1964 Fuller's domes "covered more square feet of the Earth than any other single kind of shelter." Ibid.

4. Museum of Modern Art, New York, "Visionary Architecture," press release, September 29, 1960; exhibition, September 29–December 4, 1960.

5. R. Buckminster Fuller, "Here we have the same tensegrity principles, but instead of being a spherical structure, it is a linear structure. It is a tensegrity mast at New York's Museum of Modern Art. If you study this you will see independent tetrahedral groups superimposed." "World Design Science Decade, 1965–1975, Phase

I, Document 2, The Design Initiative"
(Carbondale, Ill.: Southern Illinois University,
1964), 41.

6. Museum of Modern Art, New York, "Arthur
Drexler Retires as Director of Department
of Architecture and Design at the Museum
of Modern Art," press release, January 1987.
See also Three Structures by Buckminster
Fuller, Museum of Modern Art, New York,
September 22–Winter 1960. For a detailed
list of Fuller's creative output, see Jennie
Goldstein, "Selected Contextual Chronology,"
in Buckminster Fuller: Starting with the
Universe, ed. K. Michael Hays and Dana
Ashley Miller (New York: Whitney Museum
of American Art and Yale University Press,
2008). For a comprehensive chronology
of Fuller's geodesic prototypes, see the
University of San Diego's Spherical Atlas
Research Unit (sphericalatlas.com).

7. John McHale, introduction to "Richard
Buckminster Fuller," Architectural Design,
July 1961, 290. See also John McHale,
R. Buckminster Fuller, Makers of Modern
Architecture (New York: George Braziller,
1962).

8. Fuller, quoted in "Dymaxion American," 51.

9. Hsiao-Yun Chu and Roberto G. Trujillo,
eds., introduction to New Views on R.
Buckminster Fuller (Stanford, Calif.: Stanford
University Press, 2009), 2.

10. In an interview Stan Allen conducted
with Robert Geddes in preparing this volume,
Geddes recalled that although he extended
the formal invitation to Fuller, Kenneth
Kassler's widow, Elizabeth Bauer Kassler
(1911–98), had been the driving force behind
bringing Fuller to Princeton. A former curator

in the Department of Architecture and
Design at MoMA, Bauer Kassler maintained
a "good relationship" with Arthur Drexler,
Fuller's strong supporter, and likely facilitated
contact between the parties. For more on
Allen's conversation with Geddes, see the
Postscript contained in this volume.

11. Department of Public Relations,
Princeton University, Princeton, N.J.,
"Release: Sunday, November 15, 1953,"
press release, November 1953. Robert
Geddes Papers.

12. For more on the Princeton sphere, see
"Discontinuous Compression Sphere, School
of Architecture, Princeton University, 1953,"
in The Artifacts of R. Buckminster Fuller:
A Comprehensive Collection of His Designs
and Drawings in Four Volumes (New York:
Garland Publishing, 1985), 181–85.

13. Fuller's patent describes the tensile-
integrity structure as "a strut and a pair of
flexible tension slings each connected to
an end portion and to a portion intermediate
the ends of the strut, and means for
connecting said slings respectively to end
portions of two other components of like
construction." "Tensile-Integrity Structures,"
U.S. Patent No. 3,063,521. Fuller applied
for this patent on August 31, 1959; he
received it on November 13, 1962, almost a
decade after he built the Princeton structure.
On Fuller's patents, see R. Buckminster
Fuller, Inventions: The Patented Works of
R. Buckminster Fuller (New York: St. Martin's
Press, 1983).

14. Ibid. Regarding the principle of discontinuous-
compression in that project, Fuller later
wrote, "We manufactured and assembled a
40 foot tensegrity sphere of 90 struts. A

LÓPEZ-PÉREZ: INTRODUCTION

snowplow ran into this structure on one side and way around 180 degrees from the point of impact a member bent. The loads were distributed completely symmetrically in all directions from the point of impact until finally they came together again at the other pole. There the forces converged in full concentration as waves develop on spheres." Fuller, "World Design Science Decade," 39.

15. Fuller, "Tensile-Integrity Structures."

16. Ibid.

17. Ibid. For more on his "Tensile-Integrity Structures" patent, see Fuller, Inventions, 179.

18. "The Sphere of Ideas," Princeton Alumni Weekly LIV, no. 10 (November 27, 1953): 8.

19. Henry McLaughlin III, "Scientist Builds Model Earth in Princeton Lab," The Daily Princetonian (March 24, 1960): 1. The basic form of a spherical, or "globe," map stemmed from Fuller's belief that "as the Earth is a spherical body, so the only true cartographic representation of its true surface must be spherical. All flat surface maps are compromises with truth." "Dymaxion Map [Cartography Patent]," in Fuller, Inventions, 90.

20. Fuller, quoted in McLaughlin, "Scientist Builds Model Earth," 1.

21. James Robert Hillier, "What Is the Geoscope," Geoscope 1960, 4. Robert Geddes Papers. On the Cornell project, see "Twenty-Foot Globe of Wooden Slats, Cornell University, 1952," The Artifacts of R. Buckminster Fuller, 86. Fuller began a third geoscope, at the University of Minnesota in 1954, which he nicknamed "Minni-Earth." R. Buckminster Fuller, letter to Brigadier General Harold E. Watson,

United States Air Force, 19 April 1955. Robert Geddes Papers.

22. Hillier, "What Is the Geoscope," 4–5.

23. "I send you this letter because of your long demonstrated interest and support of my geographical and my structural explorations alike which have now become unexpectedly married in Minni-Earth." Fuller to Watson, 11.

24. "Princeton Builds a Large Globe Map," New York Times, April 6, 1960.

25. R. Buckminster Fuller, "Geoscope= World Looks at Itself," entry in Synergetics Dictionary: The Mind of Buckminster Fuller, vol. 2, ed. E. J. Applewhite (New York: Garland, 1986), 154.

26. Fuller described words as "the first industrial tools":

[I]nherently they involve a plurality of people and are also inherently prior to relayed communication and integration of the respective experiences of a plurality of individuals. This is reminiscent of the scriptural account, 'In the beginning was the word,' which we may modify to read, 'In the beginning of industrialization was the word.' Crafts are limited to a single person and involve only very local resources and very limited fragments of Earth and time, while industrialization, through the relayed experience of all people—permitted through the individualization of the spoken and written word—involves *all experiences of all people everywhere in history.*

R. Buckminster Fuller, "Emergent Humanity: Its Environment and Education," in R. Buckminster Fuller on Education (Amherst: University of Massachusetts Press, 1979), 101–2.

27. For Fuller's comprehensive attempt to codify the meaning of certain central terms, see the four-volume <u>Synergetics Dictionary</u>. For terms that appear in his Kassler lecture, see the Glossary contained in this volume.

28. In the "World Man" lecture, Fuller cites advances in telecommunications as signaling the way: "One of the great communication satellites is able, with one-quarter of a ton, to displace the communicating capacity of 75,000 tons of cable under the Atlantic."

29. K. Michael Hays, "Fuller's Geological Engagements with Architecture," in <u>Buckminster Fuller: Starting with the Universe</u>, 3.

30. Ibid., 9.

31. Ibid.

32. Fuller envisioned an "epochal re-orientation of man" through a refocusing of university education: "[F]rom now on we are going to be giving up specialization and are going to generalization. Everybody will be taught to be a comprehensivist. It is going to come naturally because man is born to be comprehensive. It is a unique biological characteristic. As he cross-breeds he becomes more comprehensively adaptive. Only in-breeding brings specialized capability, by breeding-out general adaptability. Architects constitute the last species of professional comprehensivists for they try to put things together while the vast majority, who are specialists, take things apart." Fuller, "World Design Science Decade," 98.

WORLD MAN
OCTOBER 5, 1966

R. BUCKMINSTER FULLER

JOHN F. TRAINOR, INC.
Official Stenographer
Division of Tax Appeals
Division of Workmen's Compensation
Division of Water Policy & Supply
17 Peace Street
Trenton, New Jersey

Telephone OW 5-6739

"WORLD MAN"

Dr. R. Buckminster Fuller,
Kenneth Stone Kassler
Memorial Lecture,
Princeton University,
School of Architecture,
10 McCosh,
October 5, 1966

- - -

JOHN F. TRAINOR,
By: Helen C. Johnson, CSR

DR. ROBERT L. GEDDES: This evening we are very pleased to inaugurate the Kenneth Kassler Memorial Lecture Series, a series that has been given to the University and to the School of Architecture by the many friends and colleagues and by many of the clients that were dear to Mr. Kassler.

Mr. Kassler, as you all know, was a Princeton alumnus, a Princeton architect. For many years he was the chairman of the Advisory Council of the School of Architecture and was a dear friend of many of you in this room.

It is probably a very fitting tribute to his memory and also to the intention of the lecture series that we have been able to have Mr. Buckminster Fuller join us this evening as the inaugural lecturer. It is our hope that as this series develops over the years that it will bring to the Princeton campus each year a distinguished man in the field of environmental design, the field of architecture, engineering, industrial design, city planning and its related arts. It is in this way that I think we can pay our respects to the memory of Kenneth Kassler and also to the intention of those who have so kindly supported a lecture series.

It is very difficult for me to introduce Buckminster Fuller to you because so many of you know him
already, but I thought it might be helpful if I could
establish a few of the facts and perhaps tell you a
little bit of the breadth of his interests.

Buckminster Fuller is hard to classify. He is
either engineer or architect or inventor or discoverer
or geographer or mathematician or all of these. He
was born in another century, and it seems to me clearly
that he is working on ideas which relate to the next
century.

For those of you more factually minded, he was
born in 1895, grew up in New England. His interests
since then have grown to be worldwide. For a while he
was at Harvard, and then he was at the Naval Academy,
and for a number of years worked as an engineer in a
variety of industrial corporations.

If you read through "Who's Who," it seems to start
out in a very ordinary way until, all of a sudden in
1927, the name comes out that he founded the Four-D
Company and then, a little later, he founded Dynamion
Corporation, and a little later, the Geodsic Corporation, and it clear the interrelationship between

invention, discovery, corporate activity, industrial
design and the design of the environment was something
that was growing and developing throughout these years.

Since then, under the ideas and the direction of
Buckminster Fuller and his associates, a number of
very profound discoveries and objects have been made,
including thousands -- probably 50,000, I am not sure
of the number -- but thousands of geodesic domes used
for shelter, used for scientific purposes throughout
the world. In 1961 and 1962 he was the Charles Elliott
Norton professor of poetry at Harvard. In 1958 he
delivered the annual discourse at the Royal Institute
of British Architects. In his own words he is an inventor and discoverer concerned very much with energetic,
synergetic geometry, geodesic structure and its application to man.

But perhaps the most important way or the most
clear way to understand the vision of this man in
society is by the chapter headings in his own spontaneous
autobiography, a book called "Ideas and Integrity."

I called this out in no particular order. I
thought you might be interested in the list of chapter
headings. They start out with Comprehensive Man,

Fluid Geography, Cumulative Nature of Wealth, Domes,
their Long History and Recent Developments, Comprehensive Designing, Total Thinking, Prime Design, World
Planning, Continuous Man and the Future.

It is a great honor and a pleasure for us to have
with us this evening to inaugurate the Kenneth Kassler
Memorial Lectures, Mr. Buckminster Fuller.

DR. R. BUCKMINSTER FULLER: My
first visit to Princeton after my undergraduate days
at Harvard, on my first visit here I came to the
Architectural School in 1929, and I have had many, many
visits since, and I have spent a great many wonderful
days in those visits with Kenneth Kassler.

I really am deeply moved. I am filled almost with
a mystical kind of experience in being allowed to give
this first Memorial Lecture.

Kenneth was completely committed to the search for
truth and its application, the applicability of our
knowledge, the closer we can get to the truth to the
problem of advantage for man and his buildings, developing not just the advantage but the inspiration of man
in the way in which the buildings were built. And so
tonight I am going to do my best to think out loud in

a way that would be very much the way Kenneth, I found
Kenneth would like to listen and talk and think out
loud together.

I have had a life discipline which does not allow
me ever to prepare lectures or even to think one minute
ahead about them outside of agreeing to give a title.
So I was asked to give a title tonight, and I found it
a very logical and inspiring title, just the title,
"World Man," because I think world man has already
crossed the threshold into being to an important degree.

I think all of the world is on the way to world
citizenship. Just in my own lifetime I have found my
pattern of yearly travel increasing in range and in
velocity. I now find my life one in which I really
literally live around the earth.

I am very often asked, as you must be, "Where do
you live?" People think it a perfectly logical question, and they expect a very sharp answer, as you would
answer, "Princeton." But the only answer that I can
give that is in any way accurate is to say, "I live
in a little spaceship called Earth," because for many,
many years I have not had quarters that we would call
home for much more than two months a year, speaking

cumulatively. I say almost a third of a century that
has been the pattern for my life.

I have always been a searcher, explorer for some
knowledge regarding the principles that are operative
in the universe. I am seeking ways in which they can
be employed to man's advantage. I have needed to conduct myself in a way that would bring favorable results,
and I have been very careful not to manipulate the
pattern of my engagement with life; that is, I don't
deliberately go to some place as a tourist. I only go
to places as I am asked or I am called by my work, and
that made it possible for me to read the pattern of my
increasing range of comings and goings as having possibly economic significance.

That was what I was looking for. I was looking
for information regarding what is happening to society,
so I could feel the places I was being asked to go indicated this spread of the interest in the subjects that
I was exploring.

So during the '20's I found myself beginning to
cover pretty much the eastern half of the United States,
and in a period following I began to cover a little
greater territory, but today I am going, I have circled

the earth at least two times a year, and that seems to
be increasing quite rapidly. With it is coming, it
just dawns upon you that there are very different
kinds of relationship of a man to his earth that are
coming up. I am not only circling it east-west, but
I am circling it northwest, southwest -- Australia.
I am now beginning to have about five or six summers
and five or six winters a year, so that the kind of
memory pattern, the way we try to remember events in
the terms of "That was near the spring of such-and
such," becomes an unreliable kind of pattern. I can't
think about seasons any more.

I wear two watches, because I wear one for my
home office so I know whether I can telephone them and
whether anybody will be in the office; the other one I
change for local time.

I have just been asked to write an article for one
of our national magazines. They say they would like
you to assume that you are the Building Commissioner of
the United States, and they would like to know what
you would do about the great urban problems. And so,
writing about it, I found myself saying: of course,
the only reason they want you to consider that you are

the building czar is so that you will be able to en-
force your will on others and be able to break through
inertias, and I realize, of course, that isn't a very
valid way of approaching problems, because one of the
things I have learned a great deal about are the
natural checks and balances of evolution. And I am
completely content with due process. I am quite satis-
fied it takes just so long -- there are no instant
babies and no instant anything. Einstein made that
very clear.

We have to remember now we are in a world of nonsimultaneous events. So I am not interested in being
a czar and enforcing my will, my political power, making myself building czar.

I was to assume I wasn't czar of the political
state. I had to assume some very powerful political
force had sent me in, but if you wanted really to make
a czar of building, why not make me a bigger one, make
me world czar of building? Then I said: why not make
me czar of building the universe? And when you get
to that point, then you say: in the first place, I am
deeply impressed with the designer of the universe; I
am confident I couldn't have done anywhere near such a

good job. But what I really care about is that extraordinary design of the universe, and that is what I
would like to work in.

What I am interested in is what are the designs
and processes and the intertransformabilities and
what is man doing in the universe, and what is he
supposed to be doing, as well as what does he think
he is doing.

So I said: I can only answer this question in the
way in which I assume, and all the known going type
of behaviors of the universe, and I am not going to
try to invent to a new universe or new behaviors, but
I am very interested in possibly finding out about man
and what he is supposed to be doing, and then how I
might be able to do anything I can do as an individual
as permitted by the rules of the universe, what might
I be able to do on behalf of my fellow-man's fulfilling
the functions to which he is apparently included in
the universe.

So then I said it was quite interesting to realize
the Wright Brothers, Bell and such men didn't need any
authority given to them as a czar. These are the men
who, dealing in the principles operative in the

universe and looking at man's needs, realized that they can employ the total principles in the universe, and they saw that men needed to communicate, and they had deep intuitive drives in them, if they could accelerate man's intercommunication, he might come to higher understanding, as man are inspired.

So we recognize, again, that the inventor needs no license from anyone to address himself to the problems of the humanity, and if he is not employing the principles which are operative in the universe, his invention won't work. If his invention does work, it is a facility for man. It will very probably decrease the frustrations of man's realization of his highest potentials.

It is interesting to think about inventions, because I find that there are inventions -- you could invent traps, and men have invented traps for years, or others which do restrict motion, and you might invent a prison which would restrict motion, but man doesn't have very great motion capabilities at any rate. He can only make four miles an hour on his feet, so there is not much further restriction to be had.

There is infinite room in the way of accelerating

and decreasing the restraints, so that such inventors
as Bell and Wright are people who decrease the restraints and permit man's greater permeation of his
total environment.

I see, then, some of the characteristics of advantage that are already innate in the human, and I don't
need any authority to be a czar because as an inventor
I have very much greater power.

I know that the word "inventor" does not command
the respect of society today that it may someday command. I am confident that in the days, the decades
and centuries immediately past, those who began to
develop high economic power and tended to lead man's
society as economic leaders had great effect on society,
and I say again to invest in inventions, and found
those inventions were profitable, they could also consider their investment very great -- and they didn't
want change. They wanted to get all the profits they
could out of the going machinery.

I feel during the last century or so, then, the
word "inventor" was a word which was used with some
disdain and annoyance on the part of the great economic
leaders. So that we have inherited an attitude toward

Close-up of the Geoscope, 1960

48

the word "inventor." I found there are inventors'
councils.

I have a number of patents, so that I am assessed
as being an inventor by others. They invite me to
join inventors' societies. I don't do so because they
don't impress me very much, and I don't think an inventor is very good en masse. Invention is something you
have to do by yourself.

In the Patent Office there are a large number, a
great number of applications that come from people who
are really playing a game. They are people who study
the patent cases. Patents have now been granted. They
try to make some small improvement on them, people to
whom it might be a satisfaction to be able to say to
their grandchildren that they have a patent, and put
their picture in a picture frame.

The Patent Office examiners found, twenty years
ago, almost 85% of the claims for patents were coming
from people playing games, people who had retired and
didn't have anything better to do. It's a better game
than quoits; could you get a patent? The Patent Office
was cluttered up with improvements on inventions but
not real inventions.

To be an invention it has to be really a fundamental surprise, something that can now be done by
man that he just didn't think he would be able to do.

In order to talk about our world man and talk
about him from the viewpoint of the already high advantage granted to the human being by the designer of the
universe in allowing him to invent, to employ principles,
if he can, combine them in such a way as to bring
about devices which will then decrease the restraints
on man, which will give him more of his fundamental
capacity of his own time to be invested by him in his
own free will way, freeing him from just a service to
his own processes, then addressing this extraordinary
advantage given to humanity, the privilege of being an
inventor and seeing what we ought to invent in relation
to our now-known problems, many of which great wrapped
up into big packages and phrases, such as: population
explosion, urbanism, and so forth.

I am going to think out loud with you in a way
that I have thought to myself a great deal. Way back
many, many years ago, it was about a half-century ago,
I began to play a game with myself which I adopted
just theoretically, because I had observed, as you

have, that when you are young you can pick up a little
heavier weight each day and your muscles begin to
increase, and you can build up your muscles. I said:
I think I can build up my answering capabilities,
intellectual answering capabilities by asking myself
each day a little more difficult question. I finally
got to a very big question, and I said: what do you
mean by the world "universe"?

I have a rule for answering my questions. My
rule for answering my questions has to be that I must
answer the question from experience, not from saying
somebody told me so or I looked it up in a book, and
they say: you believe this. This is the explanation.

I found as part of my experience that time and
again somebody that I knew well, with them we had some
joint experience and that my friend had spontaneously
described what we were describing a little more capably
than I could have, so I found when our experience
showed us that somebody was speaking, the person who
was speaking really was inspired with a desire always
to tell as faithfully as possible what he was experiencing, that I could include the experiences of others
whom I experienced as being faithful in recounting

experiences. I could extend the experience range
beyond my own.

The very essence, certainly, of modern experimental science is in the art of being very effective
in giving faithful account of what it is we experience.
So you could include all that kind of data.

Well, I said: I will have to answer, then, what I
mean by "universe" in the terms of experience, and if
I can't answer what I mean by the word "universe,"
then I'd better not use the word "universe" even again,
because it would be meaningless to me.

So I then, remembering I had to answer it in terms
of experience, I found the answer came by itself. By
"universe" I mean the aggregate of all of humanity's
consciously-apprehended and communicated experiences.
And the minute I first said that to somebody else,
they said, "I think you left something out."

So I said, "That is part of my experience that
you think I left something out, and that is sort of
an intuitive, logical kind of intuition that you would
say so, but I have included all the aggregate of all
the consciously communicated human experiences, and
they have included dreaming; they have included the

fact some people tell lies and deliberately, that our experiences include the fact there are continually greater numbers of facets of any subject, that the numbers of the words in the dictionary grow because we have more aspects of subjects to consider.

"There is, then, what is called a becoming, a growth, and there is change, and that is all part of our experience."

I suddenly realized this was a very powerful kind of definition. The only way anybody could prove I was wrong would be experimentally, and that would be an experience and it would be included, so I have had a great many people experience a matter of frustration by trying to prove me wrong. And in as much as my definition seems to hold up, we then can think a little more about it, because it has some significance in view of the fact that in the early part of our century the physical scientists,as a consequence of a number of very broad experiments that had been made in discoveries, began to reassess and redefine physical science.

For instance, it was my experience when I entered the Harvard community before World War I that scientific thinkers, the natural philosophers of the Harvard

community, were letting it be known their thoughts
regarding the earth and solar system and universe were
that the phenomenon entropy, the second law of thermo-
dynamics, which showed that systems always lose energy,
they felt that applied to the whole universe, and the
universe was losing its energies and running down.

What I am saying now does not include specific
individuals who had already broken away from such
thinking, but it was the going, general concept of what
called the scholarly society of Harvard that we were
in a universe that was running down and Newton's first
law of motion, which stated a body persisted in a state
of rest or coma in a line of motion except as affected
by other bodies, that the norm of the universe of really
at rest and the motions which we had experienced were
a sort of form of abnormality which in due course would
cease as the universe lost its energies.

But it was in the early part, just the beginning
of this century that scientists began to make experiments specifically with entropy, and they discovered
whenever systems lost energy, local systems lost energy,
they found it could only dissociate here by joining
there, and energies were 100% accountable. Therefore

they began to feel it was a fallacy to think of the
energies escaping from the universe, and simply had
the energies relaying from here and there, and therefore they felt constrained to formulate a new fundamental concept which they call the law of conservation of energy, which said no energy could be created
or no energy could be lost.

Energy, then, was finite, and we have then, along
with the many experiments like those of the speed of
light and the other types of observation, experiments
of inspired people like Einstein, Plant, and others.
We have developing, then, an entirely new way of looking at energy.

They said energy is finite, and the physical universe is all energy, so there is a finite, all energy,
physical universe, and a kind of equation Einstein
could write related then to this unit, finite phenomenon
energy. And the scientists who were concerned then
with the physical universe and all of its qualities
then said -- sometimes actually in words and very
often just by inference -- that there were many scholars
who were highly disciplined who were dealing in imponder-
ables, things that could not be weighed, and while

they respected those men very greatly, they could not
belong to the closed system, the club of the closed,
finite, physical universe, and they said these other
disciplines belong in metaphysics.

The word "metaphysics" had an undesirable connota-
tion in those days, because people thought of it sometimes inferring magic, and so forth, so the people who
were put in the metaphysics club felt they were being
put in a very inferior club and being made second-
class citizens.

I found it very interesting to be able to make a
definition, find the definition in terms of experience,
which is the very essence of scientific formulation,
that we are able to have, then, a universe definition
which then, consisting of aggregate of experiences,
required that we observe the individual experiences,
and we find that individual experiences are, themselves, finite, that our own observations in the sixth
cycle basis, tiny moving-pictures frames -- we go to
sleep and we wake up. Our experiences always being and
end; they are all finite. So we can say that the
aggregate of all the finite experiences is finite.

We can say, then, that this more comprehensive

universe,which includes the experiences which are non-ponderable and non-weighable, non-energy experiences, is also a finite universe.

This would then immediately give or make a closed system and give great validity to the highly disciplined activities of expiration of the greater ramifications of the universe than those that are identified as just physical.

But I, myself, find it a little surprising that the scientists who had this strong feeling about a finite, physical world do not ponder upon the fact that their own formulations, treatment of it, the mathematic treatment, that they were dealing in metaphysics in its highest degree, because mathematics is imponderable, weightless, and therefore metaphysical.

Now, without ability to think about total universe and to find that it includes also the physical universe, give some sort of strategic effectiveness to the man who wants to think about all the principles operative in the universe and tries to think as an inventor about how they may be employed, how these principles can be employed in relation to man.

Then the next question I found myself asking in a very big way was: is man essential to the universe or is he just a theater-goer to enjoy or dislike the experience? This is the kind of question that Shakespeare posed, and I finally came to a way of answering that question, and here is the way I organized my information.

I said that the physical universe, all the local systems of physical universe are entropic because, as experiments show, though the physical universe is always losing its energies locally and though they are picked up by other systems, the method of losing the energies as the stars sending energy off radially, the stars themselves are in great motion in respect to one another, so that the energies that are radiated off are diffusely distributed, and due to the continual intermotions and transformations of physical phenomena, the energies, I will say then, are released from the local systems and become ever more diffuse.

If they become ever more diffuse, they occupy more and more space, so that has been one of the observations of the characteristics of entropy.

So I said quite clearly, then expanding universe

top: Students assembling the Tensegrity Sphere in front of the Architectural Lab, 1953
bottom: Fully assembled Tensegrity Sphere

is inherent in entropy. If we didn't have astronomical observations, the red shift, and so forth, would seem to affirm the expanding universe.

In the most recent years there has been some speculation by other astronomers on the invalidity of the red shift demonstrating expanding universe, but the expanding universe concept is really inherent in the entropy itself and not dependent on the interpretation of the red shift, so I see, then, that the physical universe, entropic and expanding and increasingly diffuse, and as a mathematician would say, he describes that increasing diffusion as increasing disorder, so I said: the physical universe then being expansive, increasingly diffuse, increasingly disorderly, breaking up into more and more parts, makes me consider what kind of functioning goes on in the universe that balances this, because it is also part of our observation of the general scheme of physical universe that each one of the fundamental patternings has some kind of a complementary set of events. They are complementary sets of events and not mirror images of one another. They do succeed in balancing one another, and they are as positives and negatives that balance one another.

60

Therefore I felt that there must be some phase
of the universe that is contracting and increasingly
orderly. I said: how can you find that? And the
astronomers have had that same intuitive urge and
looked for black bodies that might be inhibiting
energies in the universe, but the kind of telescopes
they had were not suitable for finding the non-radiant
black bodies.

I said: one of the observations we can make is of
our own little spaceship Earth, and because it is not
radiant or we wouldn't be able to live upon it, and
it is receiving large amounts of energy from the rest
of the universe as, for instance, the geophysical year
indicated at around 100,000 tons of stardust daily
landing on the earth, and we know we receive an enormous amount of sun radiation and a great deal of radiation in one form or another from other stars, so I saw
that that radiation impinging on earth was not just
bouncing off it as a mirrored, polished ball, that
three-quarters of the earth was covered with water,
and the water tended to refraction and tended to impounding of that sun energy, and within the water's
biological life, and this biological life impounded

the sun energies in various ways, and the vegetation

on the dry land impounded the sun radiation with

photosynthesis. And the biologicals, in contradistinc-

tion to the other phenomenon we have been speaking

about in impounding these energies, did so with

beautiful molecular structures, and these molecular

structures were highly ordinary and completely antien-

tropic. And, the opposite of increasing disorder,

there was increasing order.

I can see biologicals in general were antientropic

and the biologicals impounding the energies began to

bury the so-called fossil fuels, these deeply impounded

energies from the rest of the universe. I saw the

earth was a pretty good system of energies of the uni-

verse that were literally being collected and working

toward increasing orders, where we find extraordinary

crystals in the earth, and so forth.

Then I said: what is the function of the human

being? I will now recite some thoughts which I have

regarding information that has come to us regarding

man's brain as it is probed, as a total mechanism here

is probed, by the neurologist and physiologist with

the use of electrodes.

We come to a point where a great deal is now known about the patterning that goes on here in the way of information as communicated and as reported and as stored and how the information is retrieved, to the point where the men who have been studying this total mechanism say, some of them say, very responsible leaders have said it is easier to explain all the data we have regarding this total phenomenon -- if we assume a phenomenon mind as well as a phenomenon brain -- than it is to explain all the data, all the data available on the phenomenon brain, because we assume this is a communication system. There are conversations that go on over the system that are not explicable as feedback of the system itself.

I am going to give you my own differentiation between brain and mind, and I have tried what I am now going to say to you on some leading neurologists. They don't have objection to it. I say they don't feel that they have enough experience as yet to say: you are right. But they don't feel at all like saying: you are wrong. And they do not feel that I am taking advantage of an audience in reciting what I am saying and going to recite regarding my theory of the difference between the brain and the mind.

I am now going to have to make some sort of a
demonstration to give you the difference. First I
take a piece of rope and I tense this rope as tautly
I know how, and the more I tense it the tauter it gets.
By "taut" we mean it is contracting in its girth, which
means while I am tensing it, it is compressing to 90%
with the axis of my tensing.

I am now going to take a compression member, which
is cigar-shaped, like this, and load it on the top,
and as I load it on the neutral axis carefully, it
tries to expand on its girth, which means it is going
to tense at 90% to my line of compressing.

It is quite easy to demonstrate tension and compression always and only co-exist experimentally. I
know there is really a superficial error that is
operative in many young people's scheming in an engineering world and world of architecture, where they
say, "I am going to use a tension system." They think
of tension as being differentiated from compression,
whereas we find, one, the tension might be at the high-
tide aspect in its behavior and the compression at the
low-tide aspect, so we see and note only the tension

or phases of some kind of an experiment, but we find
that experimentally both always and only co-exist.

I have another definition I made, what I call the
first subdivision of universe. My definition of the
universe is the aggregate of all humanity's conscious
and aggregate communicating experiences. I have a
first subdivision of all that aggregate. My subdivision is one which any one of us can make any time, the
very powerful capability of the human mind.

We can take any what I call a system, and a system is the first subdivision of universe, and a system
subdivides all of the universe, and all of the universe is outside the system and all is inside the
system.

Shirley Morgan can be a system; the earth can be
a system, because clearly there is that which is
interior and that which is exterior to it. Some part
of the universe has to be invested in the system
itself to differentiate what is in or outside at a
given moment. That is what I mean by a system.

Now then, it is a quality of systems that in order
not to include total universe, they must return upon
themselves, must return upon themselves in all

directions.

A plane would not do so. A plane would go on and on to infinity, so there must be some complex of angles in the system which add up to something less than 360 degrees in order to continually return upon themselves. So it turns out to be observable fact the systems as viewed from inside are inherently concave, and from outside are inherently convex.

We being able to discover, then, experimental concave always and only co-exist and also discover that convex and concave are not the same, because the energies impinging on convex surfaces tend to diffuse and on concave tend to contract. They are concentrated so that these are fundamentally different kinds of functions, concave and convex, and yet are fantastically intimate geometrically and always known to co-exist.

We can go to identify many always and only co-existing functions, such as, for instance, the neutron and the proton, and finally having harvested an inventory of co-existing functions of many different kinds, we can then bulk them all together and speak of them as a class of all the phenomenon that always and only co-exist, and in that you develop what we call the

theory of functions,and the theory of functions is, in
the theory of functions a function cannot exist by
itself. A function exists only by virtue of the
always and only co-existence of other functions.

Then from our theory of function we might further
go and have phenomenon which we would speak about as
relativity.

What is interesting about what I have just recited
to you is the fact that I started off by saying I take
a piece of rope, and I didn't have a piece of rope at
all, and nobody in the audience said to me, "You don't
have a piece of rope." You have all had so many experiences with so many ropes that when I did it, it
seemed so completely logical to you that I did not
contradict any of your experiences, that you allowed
me to assume I had a piece of rope. We call that a
generalization. That is the first regeneralization.

I didn't say whether it was nylon, manila, cotton,
what size, whether it was wet. I didn't have to go
into any of those special details of our special experiences, so it was a generalized piece of rope, and
it was a second-degree generalization when I discovered
the always and only co-existing tension and

compression, and third to find a whole class of always
and only co-existing phenomenon, and fourth degrees
to develop the theory of functions, and a fifth degree
generalization to condense that into the one word
"relativity."

Now, you can play a game with a little dog, taking a belt or a piece of rope, and he will put it in
his teeth and he loves to pull on it with you, and
he plays a game of tension with you and he is using
compression on his teeth and convex and concave surfaces of the teeth.

There is nothing in all of our experience to
suggest to us any little dog would develop the theory
of functions. I would say to you I am for the moment
content with the interpretation that the brain always
deals with the special case, and the little dog uses
a brain with his special case of tugging, that mind
always deals with generalizations. It is unique to the
mind to discover principles which are operative in all
the special case experiences, and it is unique to the
mind that it is able to generalize generalizations to
such an extraordinary degree as to be able to come to
one word, "relativity," wrapping up all these extra-

3

ordinary special cases.

I would then say whereas the biologicals are antientropic and develop beautiful molecular structures
out of random receipts, I would then go on to say the
human mind goes very much further in its antientropic
capability in that we had an expanding physical universe, increasingly disorderly, and I was looking for
a phase of the universe that was contracting and contracting and becoming more orderly. And in the series
of degressive generalizations I gave you, we were contracting, contracting, contracting and ever more
orderly, so I say then the human mind seems to be
demonstrated in our experience as the most powerful
antientropic patterns operative in the universe.

I found myself writing that and putting it in a
little publication in 1949, and the same year Norbert
Weiner wrote in a small publication. His resolution
was that man's mind was the great antientropy. He
called man the great antientropy, and I knew him, and
we talked about it. And we found how we really arrived
at it by quite different strategies, but it was interesting that any human being in this moment in history
would tend to follow through some strategy that would

69

FULLER: WORLD MAN

end up so abruptly at such a fine point.

Now then, if man's great function in the universe
is that of the great antientropy, then I would say all
his functioning which I have given you is antientropic,
which was really powerful and has to do with formulations of the mind, none of which are weighable. Therefore they are entirely metaphysical.

In as much as none of our experiences have ever
demonstrated any validity to magic, I rule out magic
as something that can be demonstrated, and therefore I
find no reason to include magic or open-endedness in
my concept of the word "metaphysical." Therefore I
find that the metaphysical seems to be the balance of
the physical, that metaphysical isn't just the name of
a club of people who did not belong to the exact
sciences, but metaphysical is a phenomenon of the universe that is in extraordinary balance and comprehensive to the physical expanding, increasing entropic,
disorderly, metaphysical, continually contracting and
increasingly more orderly until it comes to the exquisiteness of a single unity which has a fundamental
complementary of functions, but inherently includes
those functions in one word.

If man then is essential to the universe as the
great antientropy, the universe which is then following the same divergent, oscillating patterning we
find operative in all the universe physically, accounting for all the propagation of wave phenomenon, the
propagation of everything coming from these somehow
complementary, oscillating systems, then we say that
we also have to observe that where nature has disclosed
to us essential functions of various components of our
experience, we find nature also fortifying anticipatorily the total inner functioning by providing, many
times, great excesses of one of the complementaries
where the probability, for instance biologically, for
survival of various of the species which have complementary co-existence, where probability of survival by
means of regenerating by extending seeds off in the
wind, many times the possibility of that seed finding
the right, most suitable environments and being properly developed are low, as low probability, and nature
sends off large numbers of those seeds in order to be
sure enough of them would be successful to fulfill the
complementary inner functions of biology -- that is,
for instance, just the vegetation. And so logical

life and reciprocity in the atmosphere of the vegetation giving off all the gases essential to the mammals and the mammals giving off the gases essential to the vegetation and such exchanges as that -- and nature then providing anticipatorily for large numbers of any functions made me feel, then, that man is essential to the interfunctioning of the universe.

Then there must be many of them provided on many planets.

Then I am increasingly impressed with the observations and the surmises, hypotheses of people like Hoyle, who assume that there are hundreds of millions of planets with human beings on them.

Incidentally, there is a very extraordinarily interesting paper which has been written by a man named Morrisson, who is a professor of nuclear physics at Cornell, and now is a visiting professor of nuclear physics at M.I.T. on approaching the existence of human beings on other planets from an entirely different reasoning than that of the astronomers, but there are then many highly capable men in the field of comprehensive observation who find that it is logical to assume many planets with human beings. And I find, then, that

I would tend to accredit that, if we then see that man
is essential to the universe, because it seems, as
Hoyle would point out or has pointed out, that man on
earth has been behaving possibly very unwisely, and
he points out he has just discovered the atomic energy
in time to overlap his exhaustion of the fossil fuels,
and he hasn't learned at all to think in terms of the
conservation of the energy, he does not conduct himself
on that basis, and he has been deliberately taking out
those energy savings that have been concentrated to
this point and starts detonating them and sending them
off as energy back into the universe, and prematurely
detonating energy storage,which might be faded many
years hence, with enough energy concentration to spring
into some kind of energy detonating function.

Assuming in the interim man has learned on planets
where he is aiding the inhibition of energies locally,
that he then finds the capability to get off his planet
into other parts of the universe before this energy-
stored planet becomes the new radiant source.

Just thinking in such a schematic vein, I then
said: I see that it is true that man has argued to
himself really at very short range, not really using

top and bottom: Geoscope inside in the Architectural Lab, 1960

any long-distance logic about men on earth not thinking
about their grandchildren and great-grandchildren, or
the children of a thousand years hence. He has said
that it is much less expensive to take these energy
savings out of the earth than it is to take the trouble
to harness the winds and the tides and all of the other
sun energies, which are enormous, as daily income which
could be harnessed and turned to do the work, while
even helping to conserve that energy even more. Of
course it is cheaper to rob the piggy bank than to do
the work. If there is money in the piggy bank, it is
easier than working, if what you want is money. That
is the kind of argument man has made, that kind of
argument has been underwriting the validity of his
economics and what he calls enterprise.

Now then, as an inventor trying to think about
ways in which we might stem the energy outflow from
earth and aid in the antientropic functioning, what
might we do to possibly stay the course of man towards
possibly very swift doom, because Hoyle certainly infers
that man is in such trouble that he may be beyond
saving; he may have gone beyond the point of no return,
as it is called. I am assuming that he hasn't gone

beyond the point of no return, that there is designed
also into this system a very large safety factor to
give him an opportunity to discover his own error and
to set himself to behaving in a way that is logical
in respect to his function in the universe.

So I became interested as an inventor in always
observing this kind of total challenge with respect to
anything that I might try to find as permitted in the
principles operative in the universe that would give
man advantage in regenerating himself on the surface
of the earth, while serving his function of the greatest and most exquisite phase of antientropy.

I find great encouragement to think that it is
not too late for man to make good on earth, because I
see it also as part of the great design as we experience it that man is born utterly helpless, that the
young human baby remains utterly helpless longer than
the young of any other species. Certainly part of the
invention of utter helplessness is that it will be an
anticipatory complementary accommodation that would
protect and nurture the child, and parents have, certainly, certain drives which we identify as love --
parents have love -- but the parents are not ingenious

enough to really know just what to do for the child, because the child is going to have to breathe air, and the air is there, and the parents didn't invent the air, and the mother doesn't invent her breast. That is waiting for the child. The inventions have been very thorough.

So the parents dissipate to some extent from their drive to look out, but often their love is greatly misinformed by fears that have been engendered by past experiences they have had and by their parents before them, and so I find our customs and things we relay as logical cautions of the old life to the new life are often not conducive to the success of human beings.

So I see that the young are being born utterly helpless, and the older humans struggle along as best they can. They may be quite ignorant, but still the life has prospered, and so I see gradually as we human beings have to stand up and begin to look out for ourselves a little, that humans do begin to participate in the patterns of the regeneration of moral life and are successful by reason of the pre-existence of extraordinarily favorable circumstances and environment.

I am sure that in the regenerative drive I am
sure there are many humans regenerated. There are
all kinds of built-in urgings, and certainly you find
the male birds sing and attract the females, and there
are certainly very attractive colorings that come into
life, and I think possibly a vanity in man makes him
boast of his competence to others as part of the great
regenerative drive. I don't think he is really war-
ranted in being as bold as he is in suggesting, as I
find it suggested in all of my experience, social
experience and all the literature in the schools, that
man almost seems to think of himself as almost a hundred
per cent essential and successful by virtue of his own
brilliance and his contrivance.

I just have to remind you, as I continually remind
myself, that the word "automation" is not something
really new. It is a new description of a very old
process. I have to remind you that you are 99% automated and that you don't know what you are doing with
the supper that you ate tonight. You are not charging
off special energies to send the various glands and
they are relayed to some of those energies to make
hair and others to make replacing skin. I have not

found a human who even knows why he has hair.

I have discovered in my own way in checking on myself that I know very, very little, and I found that I am certainly well over 99% subconsciously operative. I don't have the slightest idea -- we find the problem a quadrillion times the quadrillion atoms in coordinate operation in our brains, and we have nothing to do with their extraordinary success in a conscious way, so that when I look on man in this way, I am surprised at the very little, tiny bit of area of his total being and his coordination and his participation with the rest of life around the earth.

I am surprised he makes so much a boast of this little, tiny less than 1% of his total activity which has any conscious participation whatsoever. It is because of this very small amount I find it easy to excuse him right now for errors that he has made, and I think life has built in, then, that vanity, and allow him to make some mistakes.

But now, I think, we are on a new threshold and man and universe, at least the team of humans on the spaceship earth hurtling on through space is about to begin to have to participate consciously in its own evolutionary transformation and success.

There is an extraordinary new challenge. We are
going to have to use this apparatus we have in a very,
very important way, so the kind of assessment I am
trying to make tonight is an assessment of that challenge.

Just as man, then, is successfuly developed in
the womb and is there for nine months, then he suddenly
is a very new thing to be born out into the atmosphere
and has to do his own breathing, and I think that all
of humanity is about to be born into a new kind of
relationship to the universe. That is my total kind
of feeling. I feel it very, very strongly.

I am sure that in as much as our total operating
capability, the antientropic effectiveness that is
inherent in the brain and in the intellect is predicated upon experience. We have to have experiences
where we make mistakes. As a child we have to find out
about gravity; we have to pull things. Parents know
that a child keeps dropping things on the floor. They
have to get experience about gravity.

Parents say, "Why isn't gravity obvious? Why does
he have to do it more than once?" If you think about

that from what we really know today, there are very
few places in the universe where gravity is operating,
where a human being could be present. If you were to
get too close to the sun, you are going to burn up.
There are very few places where it is comfortable
enough in the universe to have experiences with gravity.
In most of the universe there would be no gravity effect at all, so this is a very special area of the
universe where a human can get this effect of the mass
pull without being destroyed, and little children then
demonstrate to us very clearly there must be a number
of experiences before we can begin to gain a pattern.
and many of the special cases experiences, before we
begin to generalize and evolve and deduce principles
that are operative.

Therefore, I see our error of burning up fossil
fuel to this point is something that might be converted
very, very readily as we begin to understand it.

I went to a little valley high up in the island
of Rhodes this year to a very extraordinary place. They
said there were over 10,000 windmills in this valley
high up in the mountains, and in the older world we saw
man doing very well with his energy income with the

windmills and saw him sailing around the world using
the winds and not exhausting the energies of the
earth, and he has lost some of that quite beautiful
art, but I think we now know a great deal about aero-
dynamics and we ought to be able to build some very
extraordinary energy-impounding machines employing the
wind.

The head of the United States Navy Department
Bureau of Weapons, the scientific design activities,
points out that of all the sources of energy operative
around the earth there is none which is so plentiful
as the wind power; whereas the sun power is only available when we are on the sunny side of the earth, the
winds are present all around the earth over both the
land and the sea.

The only thing that has been unfavorable about the
winds has been their intermittency, but the magnitudes
of them are very great, as they are operative, and man
can get on very well with them if we found ways of
handling and storing energy. That is one of the things
he is learning to do quite well.

There are other ways of impounding energy, by
pumping water outwardly from the center of the earth,

and I think part of the new kind of a focus of attention of inventors, inventors taking the iniative,
saying, "Nobody tells an individual to invent. He
has the initiative."

In the introduction they quoted me as using the
phase "prime designer." An inventor is a prime designer in that nobody tells him to do that designing.
So I am hoping the inventor in everyone, and particularly in the university world, the inventors will
again re-attack the problem of living on our energy
incomes and the enormous tidal energies that are available.

**

Remember, we started to harness the tides, for
instance in Passamaquoddy, where we have those tremendous 80-foot tides twice a day, fantastic, the magnitude of the water pulled out from the earth 80 feet a
day twice a day, and the weight of it pulling toward
earth is mighty, far mightier than anything man har-
nassed before.

Then it was said politically this was undesirable
because the energies can't be transmitted by the high-
power lines far enough from Passamaquoddy to reach an
industrial center, so the project was dropped.

But today we have great changes in that capability because we have now entered into an era of what we call ultrahigh voltage transmission, and whereas up to now the distance we could send energies around the earth were practically about, the maximum was about 350 miles, now with the new ultrahigh voltage we are going to be able to send it 1500 miles, so places, far remote spots of great energy income could be hooked up to areas of man's high civilization needs.

In thinking about what needs to be done and the kinds of evolutionary accelerations that we have been experiencing without really intending to have such mutual experiences, I think some of the most important ones that we are going to have to deal with relate to our ability to mentally account in an effective manner what it is that we are experiencing.

I point to you, for instance, that our accounting of wealth, our social accounting of wealth, all of which accounting gives all of us plenty of trouble in one way or another when we have to deal with it, that that accounting of wealth is predicated upon several fundamental kinds of experiences of early man and certainly relates very much to something I pointed out to

Close-up of the Geoscope inside the Architectural Lab, 1960

you a little earlier as being the philosophy that was
operative at the beginning of the century which thought
of the universe as running down, and they thought
wealth was something that would inherently be lost,
and as long as you were identifying your wealth with
physical, and the physical was continually becoming
more diffuse and disorderly and was lost from local
availability, then wealth was something that could only
be identified as something that could be lost.

If our wealth is only physical, then we might say
that we would have some trouble dealing with it. I
also then point out to you that there has been no new
application of scientific discovery to the concept of
wealth in our time, and that it is then in our century
that we discovered the universe was not entropic, that
the energies only escaped from this system by joining
another system, that they were always accountable.

Therefore, we have the scientist giving us extraordinary assurance in the law of conservation of energy
that it could not be created or lost. Therefore the
energy is not going to be lost. It may not be as locally available as it was before, but it will be available again if you have the ability to travel from here

to there. You may get to the point where the energy
is now being employed. I point out then that I have
given myself the same kind of question,problems regarding wealth that I gave regarding the word "universe"
or the functioning of man in the universe, and I said
it is part of my experience that if people had something they called a great deal of money with them and
they are on a sinking ship, the money doesn't do them
any good.

I also can say something else, that my experience
showed me no matter how much wealth is accredited to
any individual or any corporation or any institution,
we cannot alter one iota of yesterday with that wealth.
The wealth is something, whatever it is it is something
that can only be articulated now and forwardly. This
gives me some clue as to what wealth may really be.

I found what I am now confident is what I really
mean by wealth. It is the organized capability to
deal with our forward metabolic regeneration, deal with
our needs. So I say in really assessing how much
wealth we have this minute, I would assess it: if nobody made another move, how many days could we carry
on, if we don't harnass anything more. So I see that

4

what I mean by wealth seems to break down into two
very important fundamentals. One is the energy which
we employ for our metabolic regeneration, and I see
then the energy as operative in two fundamental patterns, energies which are dissociative, radiant energies, and the energies which are sociative.

There are some patterns of energy patterning which
develop self-interferences, just as we can make inter-
ference by making a piece of rope and knot it back on
itself, you will pull on it and it contracts. I see
that there are patterns of structuring where the
energies tend to centralize themselves. Energies are
concentric.

I will speak, then, and classify everything we
speak about as matter as being the concentric patternings of energy, and there are radiant patternings of
energy we have in the form of fire and in many other
familiar forms of radiation. I find the radiation
energy can be reflected;instead of going into all
directions it can be beamed in the preferred direction
and concentrated.

I see, then, that the long-ago man going through
the woods, and this must have happened thousands upon

thousands of times, that a man stepped on a log in climbing over and around and found a log that they were stepping on lying across another log, and the other end was under a great big tree lying there, and they saw the big tree moving and they would go up and try it, and they can't budge that, and yet a little weight on the end of this is making the big tree lift. Man discovered the lever and learned how to use their gravitational advantage.

When men then learned, later on, to take levers and insert the ends in the unit fulcrum, which we call a hub, and had a series of them around a hub and then invented putting that hub under the waterfall and letting the water be pulled by gravity toward the center of the earth, make one lever after another to go around and take the shaft which is rotated and put on gears, belts, and later on making rotors and electric generation, at this point man had demonstrated the ability to take the two fundamental patterns of energy, the dissociative and sociative, and develop the interplay of them, which is the energy then made to do the work on behalf of man that will lead to his regenerative advantage.

51

From this point on it is man's intellect that is
of advantage. His observation, then, of the principles
operative in the universe, his learning new discovery
patterns of energy which are operative and shunting
them to the ends of the levers to do the work, so I
see that the organized capability to deal with our
forward regeneration is then, if that is wealth, then
it consists not only of the energy which is manipulated,
but it consists of the intellect which observes and
develops, then, this generalized principle and realizes
that the principles of the lever isn't just something
inherent in this particular log, but find next the log
will do it as well. And so they are able to use the
generalized principles to their increasing advantage
in their metabolic regeneration. So in as much as
intellect is a part of wealth, I then find the following. I find then that we have wealth as an interplay
of the metaphysical and physical in which the metaphysical takes the measure of the physical and turns
it to advantage and is part of our experience, that
everytime we make an experiment we always learn more.
You can't learn less.

This is an irreversible phenomenon. You may learn

what you thought was true wasn't true. You won't have
to waste any more of the small amount of time allotted
to your life in learning that theory any more. It is
learning more to learn that you are wrong. Every time
we employ our intellect we learn more. Every time we
make an experiment we learn more, which is to say,
then, that the energy part of wealth is non-destructible
because of the law of conservation which makes that
clear. The energy part of wealth is a part that always
improves and always gains, and the more we use it, the
more we learn.

Therefore I find, in contrast to the concept at
the beginning of the century that wealth was something
that was continually going to waste away, that the more
we use our real wealth, which is this organized capability, the more it improves and the more it increases,
and that we are now employing enormous amounts of
wealth of energy flows of the universe coming to the
ends of the levers that were not there yesterday.

The figure was published two days ago from the
Office of Economic Development that of the wealth being generated in one year by the western world -- that
is Europe, the United States and Japan -- the annual

wealth generated now is in the order of one and a
quarter trillion dollars to be compared with a total
of 40 billion monetary gold. Quite clearly, this
wealth has nothing to do with that gold that man used
to use as a means of exchange, and yet our accounting
system is one where our mature accountants meeting at
the World Bank in the last ten days said that they
tended, said some of their leaders said, "My sentiment
is in favor of gold," and our world's economic affairs
rest on such a non-scientifically informed sentiment
in relation to the operative factors which we discover
ourselves now to be endowed with, fantastic capabilities, because if we extend the energy being generated
in Russia and China, we add that to that western world,
we are probably somewhere in the magnitude of two
trillion dollars annually, and two trillion dollars
at the magnificent earning rate of 20% rate per year
on your capital would indicate five times that, or we
have over a quadrillion of capital venture now operative in organized capability to deal with our regenerative needs. This is fantastic in its expansion in the
last few decades, going out of comprehension by our
fellow-men.

When I say, again, to think about whether man is
going to have ability to carry on our earth, I am not
mildly despairing of the case, because I said I have
no tendency whatsoever to blame man. I have no tendency to find fault with the way he has been playing
or assess him, no fault to find with errors of love,
but I am observing that the factors which are operative if properly assessed indicate to me the existence
of a potential to deal with our total environmental
challenge which is so magnificently weighted on the
side of success that I now make the following fundamental assessment of the rates of change going on in
relation to man.

I made an assessment of the amount of work that
men do with this energy wealth in the following manner.
I did this first for Fortune Magazine in 1945. I did
it a little earlier for a book in the '30's. There is
something that we speak about as foot pounds of work,
how much work it takes to carry a pound weight one
foot outwardly from the center of the earth in a given
amount of time, and the way we rate horsepower is in
such terms. And that kind of work concept through
experimental information becomes, then, convertible

top: Geoscope inside the Architectural Lab, 1960
bottom: Students with models outside the Architectural Lab

into all kinds of other energy language, such as kilo-
watts per hour, and I find it is quite possible, then,
to take the measurements of the work human beings can
do. And such foot pound work has been measured in
armies around the earth during the last century, and
there is a well-developed estimate of the amount of
work a young man in good health can do in a year in
the way of converting the energies which he consumes
into physical work as measured in foot pounds, and we
can take, then, the amount of work that that man can
do in one year, and I will call that a one manpower
year. And those figures were in considerable agreement
between the armies of the different major countries,
so I took that and called that, then, a one man year.
And then I took the energy being consumed by various
industrial networks,and the various industrial networks
are often too remote from one another, and in years
when you could not send energies more than 350 miles,
there was no way to get energy from this center to that
other center, because it was more than that distance.
So I took various industrial network economies and took
the accounting of all the energies consumed by those
economies in a year in the form of fossil fuels and

waterpower, foods and every known source. Then I took that total energy income and I divided it by 25 for the following reason.

We find there is something called mechanical efficiency, various kinds of engines have contrasting relative efficiencies as to how much work they deliver out of the energies they consume. A reciprocating engine is only about 15% efficient. A turbine is about 30% efficient, and the jet engines up to 65%. Some of the new fuel cells get up to 80% efficiency.

Now, then, the over-all mechanics which we are using in our society today are still of a very low order of efficiency as totally operated. To such a low extent I find we are only realizing about 4% work out of the energies which we are consuming.

Therefore I divide the total energies consumed by net work economy, by 25, and it brings me to a 4% figure, and that 4% of the total energy consumed in a year by a given industrial economy I divide by manpower per year and this gives the number of mechanical slaves that are working in the economy for each human being or available to the total number, and we divide those figures by a population which gives how many slaves working for each human being.

I find way back in the 1940's in the eastern
United States industrially we had 135 energy slaves
working for each human being. I also found a very
large number of them were going into the next war,
and I found it was only necessary to have, with a
family of five, they only needed a hundred energy
slaves for a family of five, or twenty per person,
to keep up the high standard of living of a family
going with that high standard of living.

At any rate, using the criteria of 100 energy
slaves per family of five, I called that an industrial
have family. In 1900, less than 1% of humanity were
industrial haves.

After the mechanization of World War I in 1919,
six and a half per cent of humanity were industrial
haves. As we entered World War II, 28% were industrial
haves. As a consequence of further mechanization of
World War II, we are at a point where 40% of humanity
are industrial haves. We have gone from less than 1%
of humanity in a fairly high standard of living --
though if you take the highest standard known to any
monarch before 1900, it was not too good -- but we have

58

today 40% of humanity enjoying a standard of living
higher than that known to any monarch before 1900.
This comes out of seemingly nothing, and I have given
you some accounting which gives you one of the ways
of accounting for how we have had all the success so
far.

Quite clearly, our bringing 100% of humanity into
high advantage is a matter of time, and I find that
the way we have been doing this, taking care of more
and more people has to be thought of in the following
light.

During the Twentieth Century, during this last
66 years the amount of metals that have been mined,
the new ores that have been found, estimated ore
bodies, the total metals divided by the total popula-
lation gives us a figure which shows during the whole
of the 66 years of the Twentieth Century the amount of
metal per each human being has been continually decreasing, so the fact we have taken care of much
larger numbers is not because we have discovered more
metals, exploited more resources. We have to find,
quite clearly we have done more with less, and in doing
more with less have come out, almost exclusively of the

technology of the sea and air and now the space where
it has been essential to do more with less.

On the land in building a building we have said:
the wider the walls, the higher, the more protection
we felt, the greater security. But on the sea and
sky you had a fundamental floatability or liftability
of the plane, and we had to do more with less. So the
technology of developing of the enormous hitting power
had enormous fallout into our domestic economy of doing
more with less.

If we have to wait for the fallout of the doing
more with less to take us to 100% of humanity, we might
quite readily get to the point where man would blow
himself up, because if the race to date for developing
more with less capability has to be challenging a next
war, we might readily employ those weapons. It takes
22 years from the fallout from the weaponry technology
to get into our domestic economy. We can save 22
years if we set about deliberately to undertake to
redesign the use of our resources in such a manner that
we could take care of 100% of humanity.

I see these as fundamental challenges, whether
man is going to blow himself up or not or whether he

will decide on the kind of information that is now
tending to merge in our cerebrating, our pondering
whether our young world will take the initiative and
set about deliberately to try to employ those resources
by a designed science competence so the resources will
be adequate to the service of humanity.

I give one example of the doing more with less.
One of the great communication satellites is able,
with one-quarter of a ton, to displace the communicating capability of 75,000 tons of cable under the
Atlantic.

I will then end with the fact that my experience
with the young world seems to tell me they are impatient
with the concept of solving problems of man by war and
political biases, and I see the young tending toward
becoming world thinkers.

Many were shocked by the inquiry of the reporters
of the students at Berkeley a year ago, which indicated
that the young people did not feel this particular
loyalty to their families, to their university, to
their country, but it turns out on further inquiry of
those young people that their loyalty is to the world --
if not the whole world, they don't have a bias. Their

idealism is even higher, so it is my own working hypotheses right now, my prophecy, the best I can prophesy to myself is the young world is about to take the initiative as inventor-scientist, and in the employing of principles which are operative in universities immediately available to them and will succeed in converting the resources available to us to such high order of effectiveness as to take care of 100% of humanity.

Thank you.

DR. GEDDES: Thank you very much, Mr. Fuller.

I know that you felt the warmth of the audience with us tonight, and thank you for sharing this evening with us and for giving us some insight into the nature and scope of inventions, some of the personal and social problems connected with it.

I would also like to thank the Committee that made possible the lecture series by their contributions and hard work, and also the members of the New Jersey Society of Architects, whose officers have joined with us this evening in sponsoring this event. Thank you again, Mr. Fuller. Please come again.

- - -

GLOSSARY

COMPILED BY DANIEL LÓPEZ-PÉREZ

For R. Buckminster Fuller, words and concepts were intimately related. "[T]he numbers of the words in the dictionary grow," he asserts in his "World Man" lecture, "because we have more aspects of subjects to consider." Fuller saw language as an invaluable resource—as a tool to be used not only for sharing ideas with others but also for developing ideas. Language was not an end in itself but rather a discursive process, through which he created and explored new concepts. By recombining elements of existing words Fuller coined many new ones, including "ephemeralization" (the nominal form of the verbed noun "ephemeral"), which refers to the idea of "progressively doing more with less," and "dymaxion" (an adjective formed from "dynamic" and "maximum"), which he defines as "maximum output with minimum input."

The attempt to codify his core terms plays a central role in a series of books Fuller wrote in collaboration with editor E. J. Applewhite beginning in the 1970s. Sharing the word "synergetics" in their titles, the works aimed at providing a comprehensive exposition of Fuller's radical epistemological cosmos with its landscape of unfamiliar models and metaphors. In preparing the Synergetics volumes, Fuller sent Applewhite copies of all the books, articles, lectures, manuscripts, and letters he had written, together with notebooks, drawings, blueprints, and press clippings documenting his work. He also sent him two trunks full of notes he had collected for the project, dating as far back as the 1940s.

> "Synergetics shows us how we may measure our experiences geometrically and topologically and how we may employ geometry and topology to coordinate all information regarding our experiences, both metaphysical and physical. Information can be either conceptually metaphysical or quantitatively special case physical experiencing, or it can be both. The quantized physical case is entropic, while the metaphysical generalized conceptioning induced by the generalized content of the information is syntropic. The resulting mind-appreciated syntropy evolves to anticipatorily terminate the entropically accelerated disorder."
>
> —R. Buckminster Fuller, Synergetics 2, 1979

Synergetics: Explorations in the Geometry of Thinking was published in 1975. Synergetics 2, which amplified and amended that volume, appeared in 1979. A third and final book, published in 1986 under the title Synergetics Dictionary: The Mind of Buckminster Fuller, was the culmination of the effort to summarize Fuller's thinking, largely by providing definitions of the terms that had become part of his unique lexicon. Completed posthumously, the dictionary reproduces in four monumental volumes the raw materials that Applewhite created while working with Fuller on the two previous books: an exhaustively cross-referenced, alphabetically coded, first-word index of his topical concepts. Typed note cards, each containing a concept, its definition, and (somewhat cryptic) citations from the literature in which the concept appeared, were reproduced in facsimile form, some with handwritten corrections by Fuller as he worked to establish a definitive set of terms.

> "Neither Bucky nor I realized it at the time, but as all those files were compiled they seemed to manifest a sort of self-organizing character, and we ended up creating something approaching a new art form."
>
> —E. J. Applewhite, "Rationale for the Dictionary," Synergetics Dictionary, vol. 1, 1986

For Fuller, the Synergetics project aimed to "measure" all human experience and "coordinate" it into a pattern of words. Applewhite describes that discursive pattern in the introduction to the Synergetics Dictionary as "a kind of poetic combination of feeling and abstraction—physical sensations merging into metaphysical patterns." On the one hand, a set of diverging lines reveals physical "experiencing"—our increase in understanding of the physical world through the gathering of more and more quantifiable data—as "entropic," chaotic, and ever expanding. On the other hand, a set of converging lines shows metaphysical "conceptioning"—our search for conceptual order within the expansive entropy of the physical world—as "syntropic," increasingly organized and orderly. If Fuller's incessant investigation of the physical world strove to discover nature's rules, his conceptual ordering tried to "anticipatorily terminate" that world's "accelerated disorder." The physical and conceptual are brought together into what Fuller and Applewhite describe as an "epistemography of generalization," an endlessly shifting topography propelled by the interplay of all human thinking and experiencing.

The glossary of terms included in this volume illustrates Fuller's unique and extraordinary exploration of language as it relates to his Kassler lecture, delivered at the Princeton School of Architecture in 1966 and reprinted here in its entirety. The glossary lists a number of key terms, accompanied by surrounding text from the body of the lecture (referenced by page number in the original "World Man" typescript). Brief editorial notes explicate the term's underlying concepts and contextualize it within the broad network of Fuller's ideas. Interspersed with the terms are reproductions of the original drawings Fuller submitted for the patent applications which formed the basis of the two physical models built at Princeton: the "Cartography" patent, filed January 29, 1946; and the "Tensile-Integrity Structures" patent, filed November 13, 1962. Excerpts from Fuller's Synergetics volumes (identified by title, year, volume, and page or section number) are also included, as are cross-references to other texts, which provide additional literary context. What becomes apparent in comparing the many uses of these terms over the course of his long career is that, despite sincere efforts, Fuller's terminology never becomes fixed or static. Iterative and evolving, like his models of nature's laws, his definitions move and extend from one area of relevance to another; from the scale of the human body, for example, to the scale of the universe. Taken together and read in the context of the "World Man" lecture, the terms and their definitions provide an abstract but suggestive outline of Fuller's "geometry of thinking."

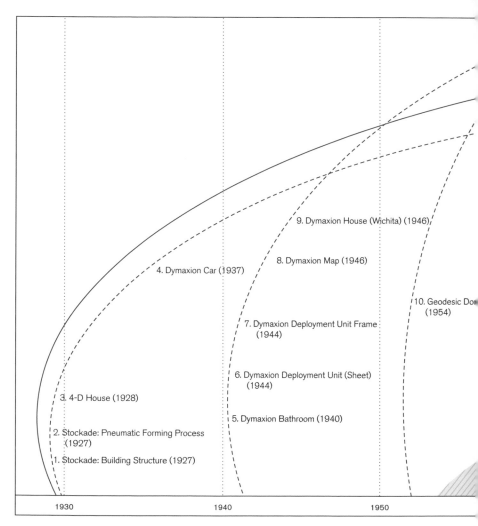

9. Dymaxion House (Wichita) (1946)

8. Dymaxion Map (1946)

4. Dymaxion Car (1937)

10. Geodesic Dome
(1954)

7. Dymaxion Deployment Unit Frame
(1944)

6. Dymaxion Deployment Unit (Sheet)
(1944)

3. 4-D House (1928)

5. Dymaxion Bathroom (1940)

2. Stockade: Pneumatic Forming Process
(1927)

1. Stockade: Building Structure (1927)

1930   1940   1950

This diagram plots the introduction of key terms used by Fuller in his "World Man" lecture along a chronological axis, based on bibliographic references provided by Applewhite in his <u>Synergetics Dictionary: The Mind of Buckminster Fuller</u> (1986). Interspersed within this chronology are a variety of Fuller's inventions, numbered as they appeared in <u>Inventions: The Patented Works of R. Buckminster Fuller</u> (1983).

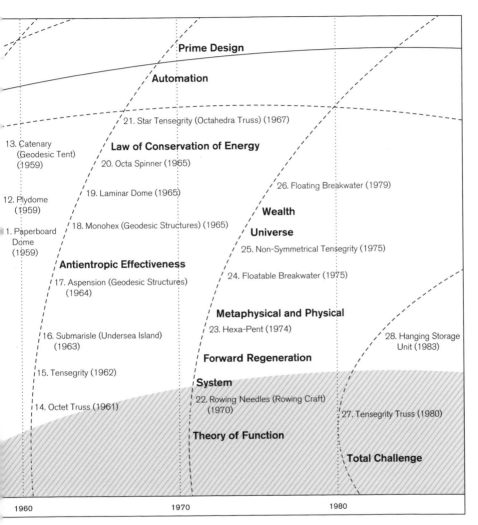

Prime Design

Automation

21. Star Tensegrity (Octahedra Truss) (1967)

13. Catenary
(Geodesic Tent)
(1959)

Law of Conservation of Energy

20. Octa Spinner (1965)

26. Floating Breakwater (1979)

19. Laminar Dome (1965)

12. Plydome
(1959)

Wealth

1. Paperboard
Dome
(1959)

18. Monohex (Geodesic Structures) (1965)

Universe

25. Non-Symmetrical Tensegrity (1975)

Antientropic Effectiveness

24. Floatable Breakwater (1975)

17. Aspension (Geodesic Structures)
(1964)

Metaphysical and Physical

23. Hexa-Pent (1974)

16. Submarisle (Undersea Island)
(1963)

28. Hanging Storage
Unit (1983)

Forward Regeneration

15. Tensegrity (1962)

System

22. Rowing Needles (Rowing Craft)
(1970)

14. Octet Truss (1961)

27. Tensegrity Truss (1980)

Theory of Function

Total Challenge

1960   1970   1980

"[T]he ANTIENTROPIC EFFECTIVENESS that is inherent in the brain and in the intellect is predicated upon experience. We have to have experiences where we make mistakes. As a child we have to find out about gravity; we have to pull things.... [T]here must be a number of experiences before we can begin to gain a pattern and many of the special cases experiences, before we begin to generalize and evolve and deduce principles that are operative."

—"World Man," 1966, pp. 42–43

In considering the relationship between physical and metaphysical phenomena, Fuller draws a distinction between the "brain" and the "mind." The brain coordinates all of the information given to us by our senses (smell, touch, sound, et cetera), whereas the mind reflects intuitively upon the implications of that information. For Fuller, "design" emanates from the search for insights gleaned from observing the physical world and its "special case experiences." The patterns that emerge are then abstracted into generalized principles.

The process of translating the physical into the metaphysical can also operate in the reverse. "Physical projections" can result from conceptual patterns, the presence of which subconsciously affects human behavior. Potential lies in our capacity to consolidate abstract concepts based on the observation of physical phenomena into generalized principles and, in turn, translate these into physical projections that alter our relationship to our environment in beneficial ways. Fuller calls our capacity to carry out this feedback process of discovery and translation our "antientropic effectiveness."

"Antientropic Ordering Principles: I think the ANTIENTROPIC ORDERING PRINCIPLES are both subconsciously and consciously developed by humans as conventions of understanding of, for instance, how we can prosper without getting into trouble. 'The Law and the Citizen' relates to this consciousness. Laws are conventions, working agreements, often different from the experimentally discovered principles governing physical Universe behaviors. There is usually a deal of difference between yesterday's erroneous assumptions and today's scientific findings."

—*Law*, May 1965; cited in *Synergetics Dictionary*, 1986, vol. 1, p. 71

Nov. 13, 1962   R. B. FULLER   3,063,521
                    TENSILE-INTEGRITY STRUCTURES
Filed Aug. 31, 1959   13 Sheets-Sheet 6

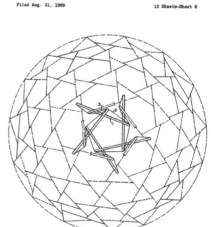

INVENTOR.
R. BUCKMINSTER FULLER
BY
ATTORNEYS

automation.

"I just have to remind you, as I continually remind myself, that the word 'AUTOMATION' is not something really new. It is a description of a very old process.... [Y]ou are 99% automated...you don't know what you are doing with the supper that you ate tonight....I have discovered...that I know very, very little, and found that I am certainly well over 99% subconsciously operative.... [A] quadrillion times the quadrillion atoms in coordinate operation in our brains, and we have nothing to do with their extraordinary success in a conscious way, so that when I look on man in this way, I am surprised at the very little, tiny bit of area of his total being and his coordination and his participation with the rest of life around the Earth."

— "World Man," 1966, pp. 40–41

For Fuller, "automation" is a process that takes place in nature on a number of scales: at the scale of the body and its metabolic balances, for example, and at the scale of the planet and its broader cosmic balance. It is also a process central to energy and resource consumption with respect to manufacturing and production. Fuller develops the term in his 1962 text "Education Automation." There he argues that education is at the center of society's transition away from mechanized work and toward an "automation" that will produce a more regenerative and sustainable "industrial equation." "[T]he more educated our population," Fuller maintains, "the more effective it becomes as an integral of regenerative consumer individuals."

"Automation: We hear a great deal about AUTOMATION as something very threatening... something new. I'm going to try to define AUTOMATION. By AUTOMATION I would mean any regulatory pattern or control operative independent of man's controlling it: that would be automated. I'll point out to you that the orbiting about Earth and all the pulsing of the Sun—this is all automated. I point out that none of you know what you're doing with your lunch right now—this is all automated. You're not consciously saying, 'I'm going to send this

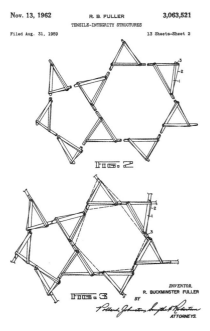

off to make hair for tomorrow, and I'm going to have curly hair,' or whatever it is. You haven't the slightest idea why you were born at seven pounds, and why you went to 170, and why you stopped. People learned accidentally that they pushed some buttons and made babies, but all the rest is automated. They haven't the slightest idea why. I point out to you that we have never had anything but AUTOMATION."

— World Game at NY Studio School, 12 June–July 1969; Saturn Film transcript, Sound 1, Reel 1, pp. 83–84; cited in *Synergetics Dictionary*, 1986, vol. 1, p. 117

forward regeneration.

"From this point on it is man's intellect that is of advantage. His observation, then, of the principles operative in the universe, his learning new discovery patterns of energy which are operative and shunting them to the ends of the levers to do the work, so I see that the organized capability to deal with our FORWARD REGENERATION is then, if that is wealth, then it consists not only of the energy which is manipulated, but it consists of the intellect which observes and develops.... And so [humans] are able to use the generalized principles to their increasing advantage in their metabolic regeneration."

—"World Man," 1966, p. 51

The term "regeneration" was intrinsic to Fuller's "wealth," a concept that went well beyond an abundance of physical resources. Technology constantly improves the efficiency and precision with which materials are transformed through modern processes of manufacture. No longer conceived as a zero-sum game that unites consumption with the depletion of material resources, Fuller's notion emphasizes the system's capacity for regeneration. "Forward" or "metabolic" regeneration implies devising more efficient processes and preventive strategies in the use of material resources, as well as a more universal distribution of these resources. If "wealth" translates into the organized capacity to deal efficiently with resources, then "forward regeneration" signals our organized capacity to find alternative ways of managing and preserving resources for future generations.

"Regenerative: Regenerative means local energy-pattern conservation."

—*Synergetics* text at sec. 600.04, 3 October 1972; cited in *Synergetics Dictionary*, 1986, vol. 3, p. 495

Nov. 13, 1962   R. B. FULLER   3,063,521
TENSILE-INTEGRITY STRUCTURES
Filed Aug. 31, 1959   13 Sheets-Sheet 10

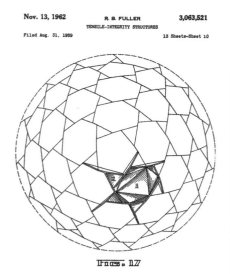

INVENTOR.
R. BUCKMINSTER FULLER
BY
ATTORNEYS.

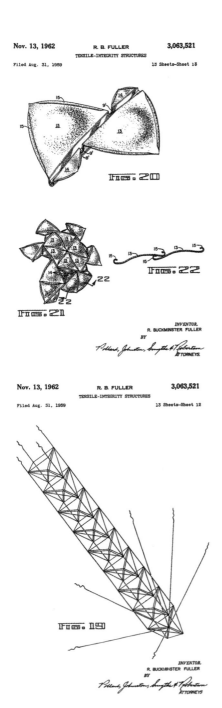

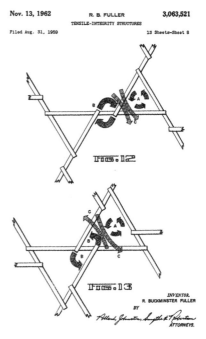

"[It was] in the early part…of this century that scientists began to make experiments specifically with entropy, and they discovered whenever systems lost energy…it could only dissociate here by joining there, and energies were 100% accountable. Therefore they began to feel it was a fallacy to think of the energies escaping from the universe….[They] felt constrained to formulate a new fundamental concept which they call the LAW OF CONSERVATION OF ENERGY, which said no energy could be created or no energy could be lost. Energy, then was finite, and we have then, along with the many experiments like those of the speed of light and the other types of observation, experiments of inspired people like Einstein, Plant, and others. We have developing, then an entirely new way of looking at energy."

—"World Man," 1966, pp. 18–19

In describing the law of conservation of energy, where the total amount of energy in a system remains constant over time, Fuller makes reference to Einstein's theory of relativity, in which energy has an equivalent mass and mass has an equivalent energy. After Einstein, the "law of conservation of energy" could be understood as a "law of conservation of mass-energy," a revision of the nineteenth-century laws of physics in which energy was somehow lost as it was transferred from one system to another. Fuller highlighted this twentieth-century discovery as a "new cosmological concept of an inexhaustible" universe, where energy can be understood as "associative as matter" and "disassociative as radiation."

"Physicists had predicated their grand strategies upon the experience of trying to make something like a perpetual motion machine. They found that all local machines always had friction, therefore energies were always going out of the system. They call that entropy: local systems were always losing energy to the rest of the universe. When the physicist began to look at their total experience instead of at just one of their experiences, they found that while the energy may escape from one system, it does not go out of the universe. It could only disassociate in one place by associating in another place. They found that this experimentally true, and finally, by the mid-19th century, they dared to develop what they called the LAW OF CONSERVATION OF ENERGY, which said that no energy could be created and no energy could be lost. Energy is finite. Physical universe is finite. Physical Universe is just as finite as the triangle of 180 degrees."

—*Synergetics*, 1975, sec. 116.00

"Energy: Scientists experimenting with entropy discovered that while energy left one local system after another, it always did so only by joining other local systems. The scientists found that energy was always 100 percent accountable. Therefore, they had to elucidate a new and fundamental scientific law which they called 'LAW OF CONSERVATION OF ENERGY' which stated that energy could be neither created nor lost.... Therefore we emerged scientifically in the early days of the 20th century into an entirely new cosmological concept of an inexhaustible, ergo finite (physical) Universe consisting entirely of energy—energy associative as matter, and energy disassociative as radiation, and both intertransformable."

—NASA Speech, June 1966, p. 25; cited in *Synergetics Dictionary*, 1986, vol. 1, p. 616

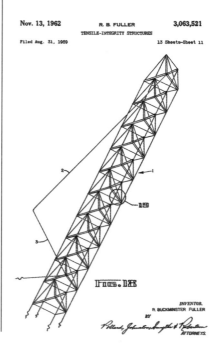

Nov. 13, 1962   R. B. FULLER   3,063,521
TENSILE-INTEGRITY STRUCTURES
Filed Aug. 31, 1959   13 Sheets-Sheet 11

INVENTOR.
R. BUCKMINSTER FULLER
BY
ATTORNEYS.

metaphysical and physical.

"I find that the metaphysical seems to be the balance of the PHYSICAL, that METAPHYSICAL isn't just the name of a club of people who did not belong to the exact sciences, but METAPHYSICAL is a phenomenon of the universe that is in extraordinary balance and comprehensive to the PHYSICAL expanding, increasing entropic, disorderly, METAPHYSICAL, continually contracting and increasingly more orderly until it comes to the exquisiteness of a single unity which has a fundamental complementary of functions, but inherently includes those functions in one word."

—"World Man," 1966, p. 33

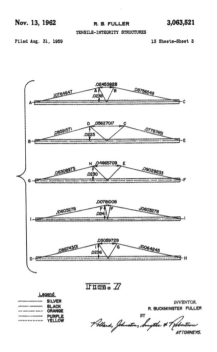

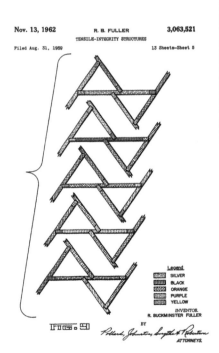

Fuller often speaks of the world in terms of dualities. Here he juxtaposes the terms "physical" and "metaphysical" as a way to describe what he sees as two parallel universes. On the one hand, the "physical" universe transcends conceptual definition and is thus "entropic" or "increasingly diffuse and disorderly." Conversely, the "metaphysical" is defined by conceptual understanding and is "antientropic," or inherently tending toward order. Using this duality, Fuller argues that it is in the balance between the "physical," as the potential to find a better "regeneration" for Earth's resources, and the "metaphysical," as the "know-how" of better managing them, where the possibility of a better future lies.

"The greatest of all the faculties is the ability of the imagination to formulate conceptuality. Conceptuality is subjective; realization is objective. Conceptuality is METAPHYSICAL and weightless; reality is PHYSICAL."

—*Synergetics*, 1975, sec. 501.01

"Metaphysical and Physical: For the support of life on our planet...you get down to two things: METAPHYSICAL and PHYSICAL. So there's the PHYSICAL regeneration and the METAPHYSICAL know-how of how to employ all the resources, all the patterns, that are operating in Universe....These are the criteria of what you need to keep a human being going."

—*World Game: Grand Strategy*, 2 June 1974; cited in *Synergetics Dictionary*, 1986, vol. 2, p. 619

prime designer.

"An inventor is a PRIME DESIGNER in that nobody tells him to do that designing. So I am hoping the inventor in everyone, and particularly in the university world...will again re-attack the problem of living on our energy incomes and the enormous tidal energies that are available."

—"World Man," 1966, p. 45

Nov. 13, 1962   R. B. FULLER   3,063,521
TENSILE-INTEGRITY STRUCTURES
Filed Aug. 31, 1959   13 Sheets-Sheet 7

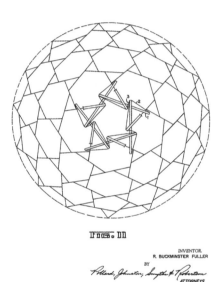

INVENTOR.
R. BUCKMINSTER FULLER
BY
ATTORNEYS.

Nov. 13, 1962   R. B. FULLER   3,063,521
TENSILE-INTEGRITY STRUCTURES
Filed Aug. 31, 1959   13 Sheets-Sheet 4

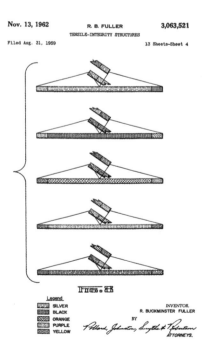

Legend
SILVER
BLACK
ORANGE
PURPLE
YELLOW

INVENTOR.
R. BUCKMINSTER FULLER
BY
ATTORNEYS.

The process of design and invention synthesizes issues of technological efficiency and prototyping with the accommodation of what Fuller describes as "ever more inclusive, efficient, and in every way more humanly pleasing performances." Inventions have the potential to transcend technical function to include a civic and political dimension that Fuller describes in his lecture as the "social accounting of wealth."

system.

"Prime Design: See *Artist-scientist*, May 1960" —*Synergetics Dictionary*, 1986, vol. 3, p. 365

"Design: Our overall use of our energy, our design, is very bad...." —*Energy Slave* (3), June–July 1969; cited in *Synergetics Dictionary*, 1986, vol. 1, p. 472

"Design: "The word design is used in contradiction to random happenstance. Design is intellectually deliberate. Design means that all the components of the composition are interconsiderately arranged; i.e., the component behaviors, proclivities, and mathematical integrities are interaccommodatively arranged. Ergo, the family of thus-far-discovered scientifically generalized principles which are omniinteraccommodative and omniconcurrent inherently constitute a design, an eternal cosmic design whose eternal interrelationships are expressible only in abstract mathematical terms. Being exclusively mathematical, they are inherently metaphysical, weightless, abstractions, which metaphysics can only be conceived of and dealt with by intellect, and being thus far apparently eternal and discoverable only by human intellect, they altogether manifest an a priori cosmic intellect of absolute integrity." —Introduction to H. Kenner's "Geodesic Math," 8 September 1975, p. 10; cited in *Synergetics Dictionary*, 1986, vol. 1, p. 470

"[A] SYSTEM is the first subdivision of the universe, and a SYSTEM subdivides all of the universe, and all of the universe is outside the SYSTEM and all is inside that SYSTEM. Shirley Morgan can be a SYSTEM; the Earth can be a SYSTEM, because clearly there is that which is interior and that which is exterior to it. Some part of the universe has to be invested in the SYSTEM itself to differentiate what is in or outside at a given moment. That is what I mean by a SYSTEM." —"World Man," 1966, p. 28

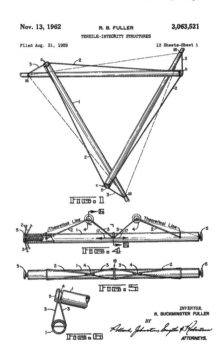

Nov. 13, 1962   R. B. FULLER   3,063,521
TENSILE-INTEGRITY STRUCTURES
Filed Aug. 31, 1959   13 Sheets-Sheet 1

Fuller defines "system" as the first order of difference and subdivision among concepts and divides the Universe into "systems," which in themselves have an "interior" and an "exterior" whose interrelationships are described as a "tracery" of lines. Following from Ludwig von Bertalanffy's General System Theory, he thought a system is any self-regulating whole capable of self-correcting through a process of feedback. Fuller used Bertalanffy's theory as a way to posit a more interactive relationship between an organism and its environment. In his Kassler lecture, Fuller refers to the physiology of the human body as a self-regulating system; in other works, he cites local or global ecosystems.

"A SYSTEM is the first division of the Universe. It divides all of the Universe into six parts: first, all of the universal events occurring geometrically outside the SYSTEM; second, all of the universal events occurring geometrically inside the SYSTEM; third, all of the universal events occurring nonsimultaneously, remotely, and unrelatedly prior to the SYSTEM events; fourth, the Universe events occurring nonsimultaneously, remotely, and unrelatedly prior to the SYSTEM events; fifth, all the geometrically arrayed set of events constituting the SYSTEM itself; and sixth, all of the Universe events occurring synchronously and or coincidentally to and with the systematic set of events uniquely considered."

—*Synergetics*, sec. 400.011, 1975

"System: The Local environment is a SYSTEM. A line is always formed by an alteration of the local environment by another SYSTEM. 'Lines' are the pattern of consequence of one SYSTEM altering another SYSTEM, either by adding to it, or by taking away from it. The event leaves some kind of tracery."

—*Line*, 25 April 1971; cited in *Synergetics Dictionary*, 1986, vol. 4, p. 114

theory of function.

"A function exists only by virtue of the always and only coexistence of other functions. Then from our THEORY OF FUNCTION we might further go and have phenomenon which we would speak about as relativity."

—"World Man," 1966, p. 30

The "theory of function" can be understood as the relationship that emerges between different networks within a self-regulating system. Fuller named the behavior of whole systems "synergy" and defined it in a letter to the editor (John McHale) published in *Architectural Design* in July 1961 as follows: "Synergy is the unique behavior of whole systems unpredicted by behavior of their respective subsystems' events."

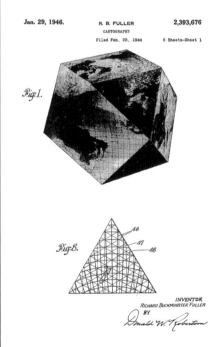

Jan. 29, 1946. R. B. FULLER 2,393,676
CARTOGRAPHY
Filed Feb. 25, 1944 5 Sheets-Sheet 1

Fig.1.

Fig.8.

INVENTOR
RICHARD BUCKMINSTER FULLER
BY
Donald W. Robertson

"The THEORY OF FUNCTIONS holds for Universe itself. Universe consists at minimum of both the metaphysical and the physical. The inherent, uniquely differentiatable, but constantly interproportional twoness of physical Universe was embraced in Einstein's one-word metaphysical concept, 'relativity,' and in a more specific and experimentally demonstrable way in the physicist's concept of complementarity."
—*Synergetics* 2, 1979, sec. 326.25

"Theory of Functions: A system is something that divides the Universe into all that is inside the system as distinct from all that is outside of it. Your body is such a system. So is a tomato can. So is the Earth. Viewed from inside, a system is concave; viewed from outside, it is convex. As the sums of the angles add up, the total is always less degrees than a plane. In order to take a flat piece of paper and make it into any kind of polyhedron, regular or irregular, you are going to have keep taking out angles to bring it back to itself until, finally, it is a polyhedron. You always come into that concavity and convexity eventually. When energy radiation impinges on concavity, the radiation converges; energy impinging on convexity diverges the radiation. So concave and convex always and only coexist. I give you three kinds of always-and-only coexisting functions: tension and compression, concave and convex, and proton and neutron. Now we can develop something we call THEORY OF FUNCTIONS where we have x and y as the two covariables and have the x standing for tension, convex, and proton and y standing for compression, concave, neutron."
—Franklin Lecture, Auburn, Alabama, 1970, p. 83; cited in *Synergetics Dictionary*, 1986, vol. 2, p. 100

"I became interested as an inventor in always observing this kind of TOTAL CHALLENGE with respect to anything that I might try to find as permitted in the principles operative in the universe that would give man advantage in regenerating himself on the surface of the Earth, while serving his function of the greatest and most exquisite phase of antientropy."
—"World Man," 1966, p. 38

Informed from an early age by a profound sense of "planetary consciousness," Fuller saw his role as inventor as improving human understanding of the planet and meeting the environmental challenges it then faced. In his famous "Introduction, Guinea Pig B," published in 1983 (the year of his death), Fuller reflects on this ambitious goal: "I saw that there was nothing to stop me from thinking

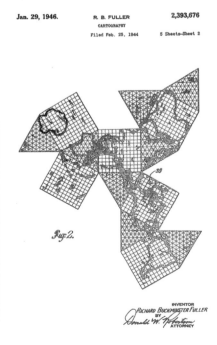

Jan. 29, 1946. R. B. FULLER 2,393,676
CARTOGRAPHY
Filed Feb. 25, 1944 5 Sheets-Sheet 2

Fig.2.

INVENTOR
RICHARD BUCKMINSTER FULLER
BY
ATTORNEY

about our total planet Earth and thinking realistically about how to operate it on an enduring sustainable basis as the magnificent human-passengered spaceship that it is." Extending his metaphor of Earth as spaceship, he urges his readers to think "about the total physical resources we have now discovered aboard our ship and about how to use the total cumulative know-how to make this ship work for everybody." Once met, the total challenge posed by Earth would give way to "the omni-physically successful, spontaneous self-integration of all of humanity" into what he called a "one-town world."

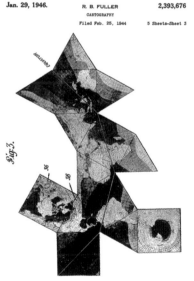

Jan. 29, 1946.   R. B. FULLER   2,393,676
CARTOGRAPHY
Filed Feb. 25, 1944   5 Sheets—Sheet 3

INVENTOR
RICHARD BUCKMINSTER FULLER
BY

universe.

"By 'UNIVERSE' I mean the aggregate of all of humanity's consciously-apprehended and communicated experiences."

—"World Man," 1966, p. 16

Fuller employs the term "Universe" as a unifying concept. Often capitalized and preceded by neither definite nor indefinite article, the word suggests an external perspective from which to test assumptions regarding our role on Earth and Earth's relationship to the cosmos. Borrowing from both the physical sciences and natural philosophy, Fuller used the term to refer to both a physical model and a philosophical concept of the world in its totality.

"UNIVERSE is the comprehensive, historically synchronous, integral-aggregate system embracing all the separate integral-aggregate systems of all men's consciously apprehended and communicated (to self or others) nonsimultaneous, nonidentical, but always complementary and only partially overlapping, macro-micro, always-and-everywhere, omnitransforming, physical and metaphysical, weighable and unweighable event sequences. UNIVERSE is a dynamically synchronous scenario that is unitarily nonconceptual as of any one moment, yet as an aggregate of finites is sum-totally finite."

—Synergetics, 1975, sec. 303.00

"Universe: UNIVERSE is the integral of all metaphysical and physical phenomena."

—Equation of Intellect (A), 17 June 1975, p. 17; cited in Synergetics Dictionary, 1986, vol. 4, p. 365

wealth.

"[W]hat I mean by WEALTH seems to break down into two very important fundamentals. One is the energy which we employ for our metabolic regeneration; and I see then the energy as operative in two fundamental patterns, energies which are disassociative, radiant energies, and the energies which are sociative."
—"World Man," 1966, pp. 48–49

In Calvin Tompkins's article "In the Outlaw Area," published in *The New Yorker* on January 8, 1966, Fuller explains that "energy, not gold" constitutes "real wealth"—wealth that is "not only without practical limit but indestructible." "Man's intellect, his ability to tap the cosmic resources of energy and make them work for him," he asserts, is what causes wealth "to be regenerative, or self-augmenting."

"Wealth: Energy is the essence of WEALTH, WEALTH being the organized capability to support life."
—*Human Unsettlement* (2), 20 September 1976; cited in *Synergetics Dictionary*, 1986, vol. 4, p. 483

"Wealth: WEALTH is the measurable degree of established operative advantage locally organized by intellect over the locally occurring differentiable behaviors of universal energy. WEALTH is an irreversible advantage: it cannot be expended in preferred reorganization of past events; it can only be expended on organizing forward events in preferential patterns."
—*Equation of Intellect* (B), 17 June 1975; cited in *Synergetics Dictionary*, 1986, vol. 4, p. 483

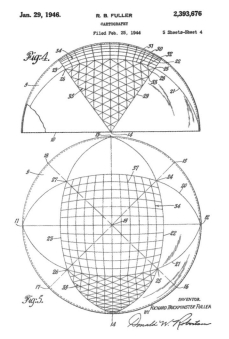

GEOSCOPE — 1960

R. BUCKMINSTER FULLER

GEOSCOPE
AIR OCEAN GLOBE
80" DIAMETER

SCHOOL OF ARCHITECTURE
PRINCETON UNIVERSITY
PRINCETON, NEW JERSEY
MARCH 1960

The following set of ten blueprints was assembled by Princeton professor J. Robert Hillier while he was a student in Fuller's experimental studio in 1960. These drawings, along with other materials documenting the studio at Princeton in the spring of 1960, can be found in a publication entitled Geoscope—1960 in the rare books collection, Marquand Library, Princeton University.

1

DIAGRAM —:- ALUMINUM FRAME

AS SUPERIMPOSED OVER FIVE EQUILATERAL TRIANGLES
OF THE ICOSOHEDRON.

NO SCALE.

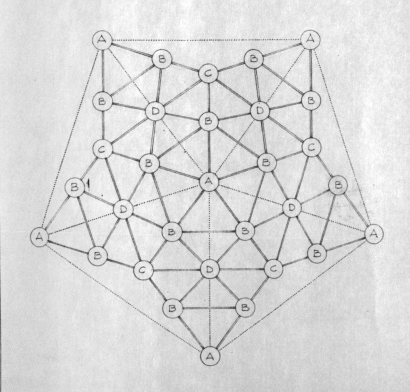

MANUFACTURING RIGHTS, EXCEPT FOR BUILDING PROTOTYPES AND USING SAME EXPERIMENTALLY, ARE RESERVED TO R. BUCKMINSTER FULLER AND LICENSES UNDER PROPRIETARY RIGHTS INCLUDING U.S. PAT. NO. 2682235 AND FOREIGN PAT. PENDING.	GEOSCOPE	STRUCTURE
	SCHOOL OF ARCHITECTURE PRINCETON UNIVERSITY MARCH 1960	2

DIAGRAM — - LAYOUT OF VINYL GLOBE SURFACE

AS SUPERIMPOSED OVER FIVE EQUILATERAL TRIANGLES
OF THE ICOSOHEDRON.

NO SCALE.

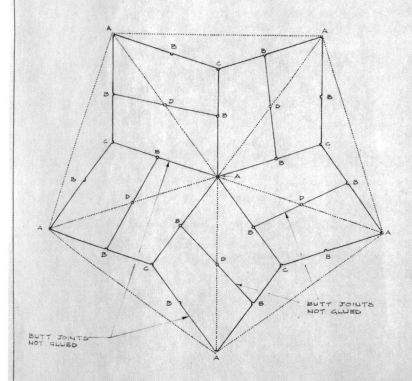

BUTT JOINTS
NOT GLUED

BUTT JOINTS
NOT GLUED

MANUFACTURING RIGHTS, EXCEPT FOR BUILDING PROTOTYPES AND USING SAME EXPERIMENTALLY, ARE RESERVED TO R. BUCKMINSTER FULLER AND LICENSES UNDER PROPRIETARY RIGHTS INCLUDING U.S. PAT. NO. 2682235 AND FOREIGN PAT. PENDING.

GEOSCOPE

SCHOOL OF ARCHITECTURE
PRINCETON UNIVERSITY

MARCH 1960

GLOBE
SURFACE

3

BELOW INDICATED ARE TWO OF 60 VINYL SECTIONS
PROVIDED TO ASSEMBLE COMPLETED GLOBE.
SECTIONS ARE TO BE PAIRED AS SHOWN TO FORM
THIRTY DEMOUNTABLE, DIAMOND SHAPED SECTIONS.

DRILL 3/16" DIAMETER HOLES LOCATED AS SHOWN SO
AS TO COINCIDE WITH FASTENERS AT APEXES OF CONE
CONNECTORS IN STRUCTURE.

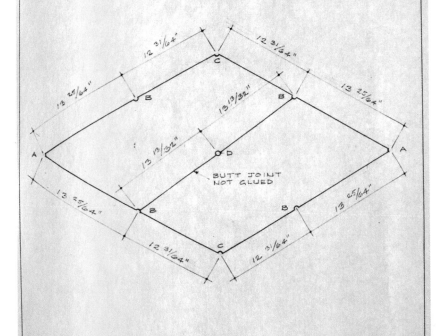

NO SCALE

MANUFACTURING RIGHTS, EXCEPT FOR
BUILDING PROTOTYPES AND USING SAME
EXPERIMENTALLY, ARE RESERVED TO
R. BUCKMINSTER FULLER AND LICENSES
UNDER PROPRIETARY RIGHTS INCLUDING
U.S. PAT. NO. 2682235 AND FOREIGN PAT.
PENDING.

GEOSCOPE

GLOBE
SURFACE

SCHOOL OF ARCHITECTURE
PRINCETON UNIVERSITY

MARCH 1960

4

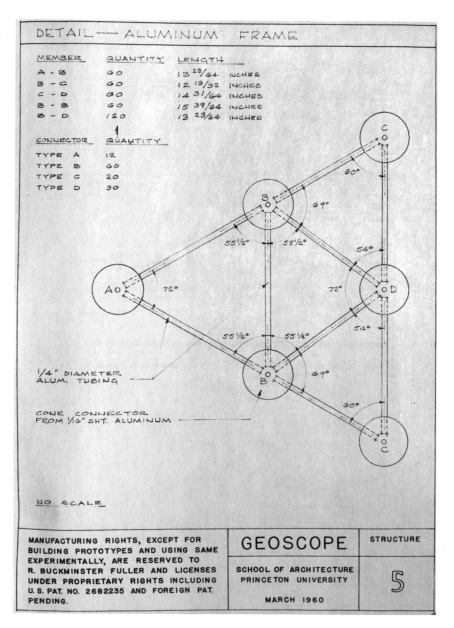

DETAIL — ALUMINUM FRAME

MEMBER	QUANTITY	LENGTH
A - B	60	13 23/64 INCHES
B - C	60	12 19/32 INCHES
C - D	60	14 31/64 INCHES
B - B	60	15 39/64 INCHES
B - D	120	13 23/64 INCHES

CONNECTOR	QUANTITY
TYPE A	12
TYPE B	60
TYPE C	20
TYPE D	30

C

60°

B

69°

55½° 55½°

54°

A 72° 72° D

54°

55½° 55½°

B 69°

1/4" DIAMETER ALUM. TUBING

60°

CONE CONNECTOR FROM 1/16" SHT. ALUMINUM

C

NO SCALE

MANUFACTURING RIGHTS, EXCEPT FOR BUILDING PROTOTYPES AND USING SAME EXPERIMENTALLY, ARE RESERVED TO R. BUCKMINSTER FULLER AND LICENSES UNDER PROPRIETARY RIGHTS INCLUDING U. S. PAT. NO. 2682235 AND FOREIGN PAT. PENDING.

GEOSCOPE

SCHOOL OF ARCHITECTURE
PRINCETON UNIVERSITY

MARCH 1960

STRUCTURE

5

FULL SCALE SECTION THRU JOINT AT CONE

REQUIRED HARDWARE

1440	NO. 4-40 ALUMINUM MACHINE SCREWS 1/2" LONG WITH 1440 HEXAGONAL NUTS & 2880 WASHERS
122	NO. 6-32 MACHINE SCREWS 3" LONG WITH 122 HEXAGONAL NUTS
122	WING NUTS FOR 6-32 MACHINE SCREW
122	STEEL 'TEENUTS' TO RECEIVE 6-32 MACHINE SCREW
244	LOCK WASHERS

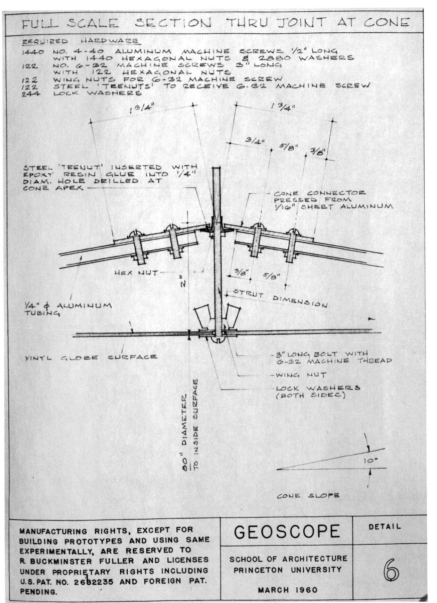

STEEL 'TEENUT' INSERTED WITH EPOXY RESIN GLUE INTO 1/4" DIAM. HOLE DRILLED AT CONE APEX

1 3/4"

1 3/4"

3/4" 5/8" 3/8"

CONE CONNECTOR PRESSED FROM 1/16" SHEET ALUMINUM

HEX NUT — No. 2

3/8" 5/8"

STRUT DIMENSION

1/4" φ ALUMINUM TUBING

VINYL GLOBE SURFACE

80" DIAMETER TO INSIDE SURFACE

3" LONG BOLT WITH 6-32 MACHINE THREAD

WING NUT

LOCK WASHERS (BOTH SIDES)

10°

CONE SLOPE

MANUFACTURING RIGHTS, EXCEPT FOR BUILDING PROTOTYPES AND USING SAME EXPERIMENTALLY, ARE RESERVED TO R. BUCKMINSTER FULLER AND LICENSES UNDER PROPRIETARY RIGHTS INCLUDING U.S. PAT. NO. 2682235 AND FOREIGN PAT. PENDING.

GEOSCOPE

SCHOOL OF ARCHITECTURE
PRINCETON UNIVERSITY

MARCH 1960

DETAIL

6

F. S. DETAIL — CONE CONNECTOR TYPE A

CONE CONNECTOR
PRESSED FROM
1/16" SHEET ALUMINUM
REQUIRED: 12 AS SHOWN
72°
72°
72°
72°
72°
HOLES DRILLED
TO RECEIVE NO. 4-40
ALUMINUM MACHINE
SCREWS
1/4" DIAMETER
HOLE DRILLED TO
RECEIVE STEEL
'TEENUT'
1/4" ROUND
ALUMINUM TUBE STRUTS

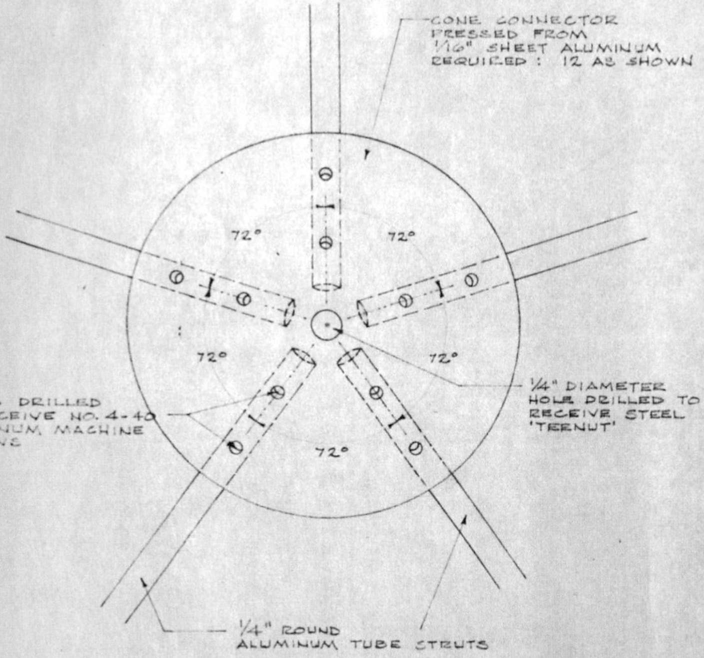

MANUFACTURING RIGHTS, EXCEPT FOR BUILDING PROTOTYPES AND USING SAME EXPERIMENTALLY, ARE RESERVED TO R. BUCKMINSTER FULLER AND LICENSES UNDER PROPRIETARY RIGHTS INCLUDING U.S. PAT. NO. 2682235 AND FOREIGN PAT. PENDING.	GEOSCOPE SCHOOL OF ARCHITECTURE PRINCETON UNIVERSITY MARCH 1960	DETAIL 7

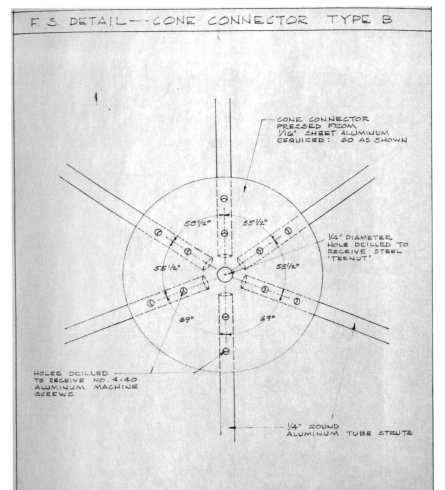

CONE CONNECTOR
PRESSED FROM
1/16" SHEET ALUMINUM
REQUIRED: 60 AS SHOWN

1/4" DIAMETER
HOLE DRILLED TO
RECEIVE STEEL
'TEENUT'

55 1/2°   55 1/2°

55 1/2°   55 1/2°

69°   69°

HOLES DRILLED
TO RECEIVE NO. 4-40
ALUMINUM MACHINE
SCREWS

1/4" ROUND
ALUMINUM TUBE STRUTS

MANUFACTURING RIGHTS, EXCEPT FOR BUILDING PROTOTYPES AND USING SAME EXPERIMENTALLY, ARE RESERVED TO R. BUCKMINSTER FULLER AND LICENSES UNDER PROPRIETARY RIGHTS INCLUDING U. S. PAT. NO. 2682235 AND FOREIGN PAT. PENDING.

GEOSCOPE	DETAIL
SCHOOL OF ARCHITECTURE PRINCETON UNIVERSITY	8
MARCH 1960	

F. S. DETAIL — CONE CONNECTOR TYPE C

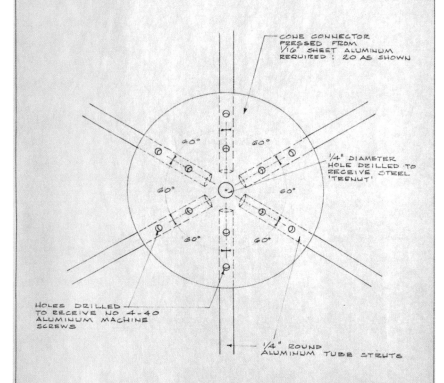

CONE CONNECTOR
PRESSED FROM
1/16" SHEET ALUMINUM
REQUIRED : 20 AS SHOWN

90°

60°

60°

1/4" DIAMETER
HOLE DRILLED TO
RECEIVE STEEL
'TEENUT'

60°

60°

60°

60°

HOLES DRILLED
TO RECEIVE NO 4-40
ALUMINUM MACHINE
SCREWS

1/4" ROUND
ALUMINUM TUBE STRUTS

MANUFACTURING RIGHTS, EXCEPT FOR BUILDING PROTOTYPES AND USING SAME EXPERIMENTALLY, ARE RESERVED TO R. BUCKMINSTER FULLER AND LICENSES UNDER PROPRIETARY RIGHTS INCLUDING U. S. PAT. NO. 2682235 AND FOREIGN PAT. PENDING.

GEOSCOPE

SCHOOL OF ARCHITECTURE
PRINCETON UNIVERSITY

MARCH 1960

DETAIL

F. S. DETAIL - CONE CONNECTOR TYPE D

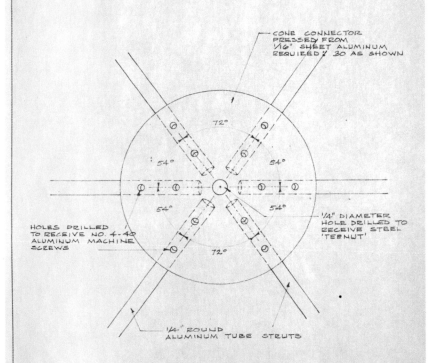

CONE CONNECTOR
PRESSED FROM
1/16" SHEET ALUMINUM
REQUIRED: 30 AS SHOWN

72°

54°   54°

54°   54°

HOLES DRILLED
TO RECEIVE NO. 4-40
ALUMINUM MACHINE
SCREWS

72°

1/4" DIAMETER
HOLE DRILLED TO
RECEIVE STEEL
'TEENUT'

1/4" ROUND
ALUMINUM TUBE STRUTS

MANUFACTURING RIGHTS, EXCEPT FOR
BUILDING PROTOTYPES AND USING SAME
EXPERIMENTALLY, ARE RESERVED TO
R. BUCKMINSTER FULLER AND LICENSES
UNDER PROPRIETARY RIGHTS INCLUDING
U. S. PAT. NO. 2682235 AND FOREIGN PAT.
PENDING.

GEOSCOPE	DETAIL
SCHOOL OF ARCHITECTURE PRINCETON UNIVERSITY	10
MARCH 1960	

POSTSCRIPT: R. BUCKMINSTER FULLER AND LOUIS I. KAHN

STAN ALLEN

ROBERT GEDDES: Lou and Bucky had a very close relationship at Yale. In fact, Bucky spoke at Lou's funeral.

STAN ALLEN: Really?

GEDDES: We talked about Lou then. And I think that Bucky had an extraordinary influence on Lou philosophically.

The other aspect about Lou I think was that he was trying to create architecture that was really comprehensive. I mean, just the way Bucky talks about comprehensive invention, or oneness, that really was the essence of Lou. I think they were very close — it was a kinship between those two.

—Robert Geddes and Stan Allen, in conversation, 2012

The existence of a close friendship between R. Buckminster Fuller and Louis I. Kahn may come as a surprise to many people (as it did to me). The work of these two giant figures of twentieth-century architecture has little in common. Perhaps more than any other architect of the recent past, Kahn is identified with solidity, weight, and mass. His is an architecture wedded to the ground: "I draw a building from the ground up because that's the way it is constructed. It depends on gravity. You begin with the way the weights can be distributed on the land, and then you build up."[1] Fuller was, by contrast, a maverick polymath who famously asked, "Madam, do you know what your house weighs?"[2] He insisted that the urgent social and environmental challenges facing mankind in the twentieth century required a break with the past; only by starting from scratch and ignoring conventional boundaries

between disciplines would it be possible to produce new solutions. Kahn, who had a copy of Piranesi's Campo Marzio pinned above his drawing table, saw his work as a continuing conversation with history. Deeply aware of the ways in which traditional building techniques had shaped the architecture of the past, Kahn was searching for ways to use contemporary technology to realize an architecture that had the same authentic relationship to its means of construction. His origins were

Louis Kahn, arches under Presidential Square, Dacca, Bangladesh, 1962–83

in the fine arts, and he had a deep connection to architecture's traditional tools, drawing in particular.

For Fuller, the areas of expertise defined by conventional disciplines (architecture, engineering, industrial design, ecology, cartography, etc.) were simply an impediment to invention. His greatest achievements often happened in the space between disciplines. Kahn is, by contrast, shaped by the discipline—by his Beaux-Arts training with Paul Philippe Cret, by his stay at the American Academy in Rome, and by his devotion to history. After Kahn, we think of tectonics, materiality, detail, space, and order differently; after Fuller, we think of the task of the architect differently.

Yet Kahn and Fuller shared a friendship dating back to the 1930s. Both were stubbornly individualistic and held an optimistic belief in the perfectibility of mankind. Robert Geddes points to a shared interest in geometry and Fuller's influence on Kahn's philosophy. This rings true; both had a deep intellectual curiosity, a speculative intelligence, and an aspiration to universality. Similar worldviews can take different forms, as they do in the case of Kahn and Fuller. But the Fuller connection also serves to open up our thinking about Kahn, moving us away from the reductive view of Kahn

as the poetic avatar of "silence and light" to reveal a more complex idea of what constitutes architectural knowledge.

To say that Kahn and Fuller share a preoccupation with geometry is, however, to say very little. All architects work with geometry. It is the medium through which abstract ideas become real; everything in architecture must pass through the filter of geometry. Some architects make geometry more thematic, though, and both Kahn and Fuller used geometry very explicitly. But the geometries they worked with and the ways in which they worked with them are very different. The differences are telling. Their divergent ideas about geometry illuminate larger, more fundamental differences.

<u>01</u>

"Ferro-concrete architecture may be likened to the plastic cocoon of the archaic worm from which will emerge the 4-D butterfly."
—R. Buckminster Fuller, <u>Your Private Sky</u>

Fuller works with geometry in its purest state. Geometry for Fuller is lines of force and resistance: a diagram of performance. Geometry fosters abstract thought at the same time as it provides a powerful problem-solving tool. Calculable and verifiable, unburdened by history or symbolism, it delineates the shortest path from analysis to solution. In one sense, some of Fuller's best-known inventions are pure geometry. The geodesic dome,

Fuller with polyhedral models, photographed by Nancy Newhall, 1948

Marine Corps lifting Fuller's 30-foot
wood and plastic dome at Orphan's Hill,
North Carolina, 1954

active, vectorial force, and through geometric manipulation it can be shaped and redirected. Geometry is what allows him to do "more with less."

Kahn, by contrast, is an architect of compression, for whom material choices are laden with meaning and architectural consequence. Compression thematizes weight and mass. It is self-limiting, because mass adds weight, which in turn requires additional mass. The architectural repertoire of compression is fixed: walls, columns, arches, and vaults. All of these appear in Kahn's work. His geometries are elemental: squares, circles, and triangles, built up according to the load-bearing logic of compression into cubes, cylinders, or pyramids. Kahn is an architect of addition. He adds one element to another to create a larger whole in which the parts always retain their autonomy. Fuller, on the other hand, is a designer of abstract geometric frameworks, expansive

for example, is a geometric principle indifferent to its material realization. Domes can and have been built out of steel, cardboard, plywood, fabric, plastics, and even venetian blinds. They have been realized as highly engineered space frames or constructed out of recycled sheet metal from junked cars. As an engineer, Fuller could hardly ignore gravity, but he liked things that could be turned upside down and still function. The tensegrity mast is a brilliant example of a structural principle that seems to defy gravity. By resisting gravity not with mass but with geometry traced in wires and struts, the effect of weightlessness is achieved. The principle works equally well in all directions: "It has no top, bottom or sides, and could be placed into orbit."[3] For Fuller, gravity is an

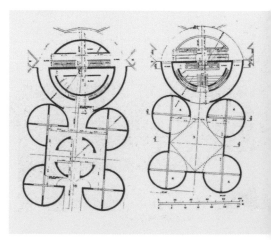

above: Fuller and Venetian Blind Dome, with Elaine de Kooning, Josef Albers, and others at Black Mountain College, 1948

Kahn, Mosque at the National Assembly of Bangladesh, Dacca, plans

and complete in themselves. For Kahn, the built work is definitive, and drawing is a means to conceive the building. For Fuller, each realization is just one among many possible exemplars of the geometric principles contained in the drawing. There is no definitive "work of architecture" for Fuller, only full-scale prototypes and working models.

Kahn's metaphysics of "order" implies a deeper logic to geometry, beyond formal composition or symbolism. The role of the architect for Kahn is not invention so much as discovery—to uncover and make visible the fundamental ordering principles of elemental geometry. His aspiration is beyond the momentary and the circumstantial toward timelessness; for Kahn, "archaic" is a positive value. This is what gives some of his buildings (especially his late work) the quality of ruins. Note the way in which all the signs of contemporary technology or occupation, such as window frames and glazing, are pushed back from the surface so that only the hard materials that can persist over time remain visible. What Kahn and Fuller share is an aspiration to universality, to an architecture that has an impact beyond its immediate circumstance. But Kahn's metaphysics of the eternal contrasts with Fuller's mystical faith in the power of technology and invention to transform human habitation.

"And specifically what Fuller had us working on, I remember, were really two things. One was geometry and the other was performance."
—Robert Geddes, on Fuller's teaching methods

Just as Fuller and Kahn use geometry in different ways, they think about program and performance differently. A telling anecdote: A friend of mine grew up in a geodesic dome in Northern California. She liked to tell the story of the escalating paranoia provoked by a teenage LSD experiment in a house with no corners. In a geometric space designed for maximum domestic efficiency, there is no place to hide. It's an extreme example, but it underscores the limits of Fuller's emphasis on geometry and performance. Performance implies optimization for one thing at a time and may not account for the full range of human experience. Contrast that to Kahn's observation that

Tensegrity mast, Museum of Modern Art, New York, 1959. Fuller's North Carolina State University workshop constructed the mast in 1950.

"architecture must have bad spaces as well as good spaces."[4] For Kahn, the building is conceived as a fixed stage for the messy drama of human activity. This is in part what made Kahn such an effective architect of buildings for collective, institutional programs. He had a certain faith in the idea that people working together could solve problems, whether in a laboratory or a parliament, and that the right architectural framework could encourage that collaboration. This is the social principle expressed by his formal strategy of part-to-whole aggregation: individuals coming together to form a larger whole, a focused collective, in which each voice can still be heard. He is an architect of "group form," and it is not accidental that some of his most important buildings and projects are for churches and synagogues.[5]

03

"Lou and Bucky did not really communicate since they spoke such different creative languages. Bucky worked with pure geometric forms but not with geometry as an underlying principle for a variety of tangible architectural expressions."

—Anne Tyng, introduction to Louis Kahn to Anne Tyng: The Rome Letters, 1953–54

If there is a missing link in the story of Fuller and Kahn, it is Anne Griswold Tyng. Kahn's employee, collaborator (and lover), Tyng made significant contributions to the work of the office during the years that they worked together. Tyng met Fuller in 1949, and he often referred to her as "Kahn's geometrical strategist." In the projects Tyng was involved in—the Yale University Art Gallery (1951–53) and the City Tower project (1951–58)—Kahn comes closest to Fuller's geometric sensibility. In the City Tower, for the first (and last) time in Kahn's work, a lightweight, basketlike lattice of linear structural elements appears in place of the closed vocabulary of geometric solids. The tower weaves back and forth, as dictated by a triangulated structural logic, rather than extruding directly up from the plan geometries. In fact, there is no plan at all, at least not in the classical sense of the plan as the formal disposition of spaces: the tower's plan is simply a horizontal section of a continuous spatial matrix within which no single orientation is primary. In another departure from Kahn's usual practice, the entire structure perches on thin legs, lifting off the ground to create an open public space below.

The collaborations with Tyng are Kahn's nearest approximation of Fuller's lightweight, triangulated geometries.[6] But even in these, Kahn's sense of placemaking tempers Fuller's drive toward abstraction and universality. In his treatment of the

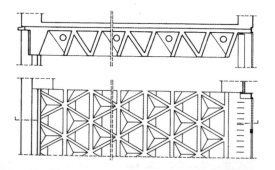

Kahn, Yale University Art Gallery, New Haven, Connecticut, 1951– 53, section and plan detail of the tetrahedral concrete slab

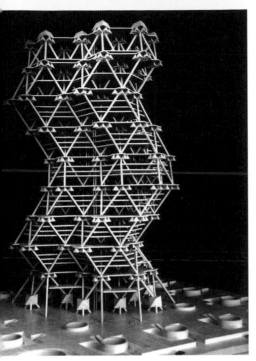

refining the design and lobbying for a commission. Clearly Tyng was the catalyst to moving Kahn out of his comfort zone in this instance, but the ground had been prepared, perhaps precisely through his long friendship with Fuller and their shared interest in geometry. As in Fuller's work, the way in which these geometries resonate with natural form provides a secure philosophical underpinning. Tyng, Kahn later wrote, "knows the aesthetic implications of the geometry inherent in biological structures bringing us in touch with the edge between the measurable and the unmeasurable."[7]

04

"In fact Bucky saw himself first of all as in inventor; I don't think he thought of himself as a designer at all in the way that architects did."
—Robert Geddes

In the end, Kahn and Fuller left distinct legacies. Fuller was a futurist, and technological change has cast him in a new light. Today he has become a point of departure for alternative practices that, often with the aid of advanced computer technology, look to solve a wide range of problems associated with the built environment. "Bucky Fuller was no architect," said Philip Johnson, confirming Geddes's assessment. "He was an inventor and a guru and a poet."[8] This multivalence has come to define his character. Fuller did not so much drill

base, Kahn designed an elevated public forum with a series of austere circular enclosures. In the final version of the project, the shear caps are multiplied and exaggerated to create "hollow capitals." This is pure Kahn: a way to accommodate modern building services and incorporate structural shear caps within a hollowed-out fragment of classical architecture. It is his version of doing "more with less." Visually, the caps create a rhythmic counterpoint to the continuous geometries of the triangulated frame.

The project, which was never realized, exists in a number of versions, created as Kahn and Tyng tested site and program,

Kahn and Anne Tyng, City Tower, 1956–57, model

down into one specific area of expertise as link knowledge across fields. His idea of the task of the architect was an expansive one, encompassing any field that might touch on technology, building, or the environment. Conventional architectural programs played a relatively small role in his thinking; instead, architecture for Fuller implied a fundamental, ground-up redesign of the structures of living, the organization of the building industry, and the allocation of resources. This is what made him so attractive to the counter-culture in the 1960s and what makes him a model for those who want to invest contemporary practice with a broader relevance in times of environmental, social, and urban crisis.

Kahn's legacy, by contrast, resides primarily within architecture as a discipline. His entire career was devoted to finding architecture's core. Stripping away the inessential, he went in search of a kind of degree zero of architecture. He left us with enduring ideas of material, tectonics, detail, and order, embodied in buildings, drawings, and projects. His written and spoken pronouncements, while often obscure, have a kind of stubborn poetry about them. His working concepts such as "served" and "servant" spaces have entered the everyday lexicon of practice. Thanks to his influence on Robert Venturi, he has been identified as a precursor of postmodernism.[9] Equally, advocates of reductive geometries and sober tectonics, such as Tadao Ando, claim Kahn's work as foundational. Whenever architects juxtapose simplified plan figures in tensely calibrated relationships, as does John Hejduk in his early work, Kahn's metaphysics of order is inevitably evoked. Beyond these specific disciplinary references, Kahn needs to be recognized as an architect of evocative civic spaces. His greatest contribution is in reshaping the architecture of public institutions and their urban framework.

Chuck Hoberman, expanding geodesic dome, 20-foot diameter, machined aluminum, 1991

His elemental geometries and part-to-whole compositions create spaces that resonate with the public and tangibly connect the present to the past. That his work can sponsor such distinctive legacies is the measure of its depth and complexity.

Paradoxically, it is precisely Kahn and Fuller's shared interest in geometry that reveals their starkest difference. For Fuller, the abstract, mathematical character of geometry allows him to range across a wide variety of disciplines. Everything that geometry touches—cartography, engineering, demographics, urbanism, architecture, industrial design—is made available through calculation and geometric drawing. Kahn, by contrast, sees geometry as a fundamental architectural property. Geometry is what endows architecture with universal intelligibility; it is accessible to everyone. The timeless character of Kahn's public buildings is achieved through geometries that are shared by architectures ancient and modern.

Both Fuller and Kahn took the long view. An overarching aspiration to test each specific case against a general principle guided their parallel endeavors. Each sought to elevate his life's work above the circumstantial. For Fuller, this was achieved through science and mathematics and an expansive, interconnected worldview. He saw everything from the Dymaxion House (1920s–1945) to Spaceship Earth (1968) as a manifestation of basic principles of synergy, nested structure, and geometric order. Kahn, too, saw architecture as a manifestation of a deeper order, in his case of the elemental geometries that link past and present. Like Fuller's friendship with John Cage (another case of close, personal affiliation and divergent artistic sensibilities), the mutual attraction between Kahn and Fuller is not necessarily reflected in the specifics of the work. At a decisive moment, Fuller exercised an important influence on Kahn, but it is also true that Kahn translated those ideas into his own idiom. Kahn's example, on the other hand, illuminates Fuller's work primarily by contrast. It is perhaps a necessary counterpoint, marking out the limits of Fuller's engagements with geometry and architecture's disciplinary structure.

John Hejduk, One-Half House, 1965, second floor plan

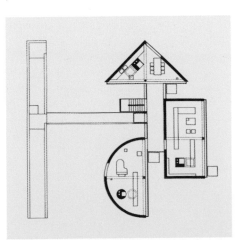

NOTES

All statements by Robert Geddes are taken from an interview conducted in Princeton, New Jersey, on November 9, 2012. During my final year as dean of the School of Architecture at Princeton, I sat down with Geddes, professor emeritus and dean of the school from 1965 to 1982, to discuss his memories of Fuller's 1966 Kassler lecture. Geddes had participated in Fuller's studios at the Massachusetts Institute of Technology while a student at the Harvard Graduate School of Design in the late 1940s. During the late 1950s and early 1960s, Geddes taught architecture and urban design alongside Louis Kahn at the University of Pennsylvania. At the time of our interview, I was struck by his description of a close sympathy between Kahn and Fuller. This essay is the result.

1. Louis I. Kahn, quoted in Michael Merrill, Louis Kahn: Drawing to Find Out. The Dominican Motherhouse and the Patient Search for Architecture (Baden, Germany: Lars Müller, 2010), 78.

2. R. Buckminster Fuller, paraphrased in Reyner Banham, "A Home Is Not a House," Art in America 2 (April 1965): 111.

3. Kenneth Snelson, quoted online at tensegrity.wikispaces.com/Fuller,+Richard +Buckminster. Accessed May 20, 2013.

4. Louis I. Kahn, quoted in Robert Venturi, Complexity and Contradiction in Architecture (New York: Museum of Modern Art, 1966), 25.

5. Geddes refers to the concept of "group form" to emphasize Kahn's close attention to community in contrast to Fuller's celebration of individual self-reliance: "Now there my recollection of [Fuller] was that he really wanted to create autonomous man.... There was a great interest in the Dymaxion House, which was related to the idea of an autonomous, self-supporting, self-sufficient individual. Now for me that was always a problem, because if one comes to think of group form, of community form—a community either of objects or buildings or activities— the notion of autonomy is antithetical to that. I think that his real dream would have been to figure out some way to build a structure that you could bring in by helicopter and that would then support itself forever from that point on." On group form, see also Fumihiko Maki, "Investigations in Collective Form," Publication of the School of Architecture, Washington University, St. Louis, Missouri, June 1964.

6. Another significant convergence around Kahn and Tyng is the work of the engineer Robert Le Ricolais, their colleague at the University of Pennsylvania, who is sometimes referred to as the "father of spatial struc- tures." See Sarah Williams Goldhagen, Louis Kahn's Situated Modernism (New Haven: Yale University Press, 2001). In chapter 3, "Techno-Organic Symbols of Community," she details the interplay between Kahn, Tyng, Fuller, and Le Ricolais and their shared interests in complex geom- etries and latticelike structures in nature.

7. The question of credit needs to be addressed, especially given the gender politics of the time. With regard to the City Tower, Tyng's recollection is definitive: "The tower is really just something I did. Bob Venturi had recently joined the office and he did a lot of work on the base of the tower. Lou also worked on the base, so he didn't have much to do with the tower either.

He didn't really grasp the geometry that well." Anne Tyng, quoted in Srdjan Jovanovic Weiss, "The Life Geometric," Domus 947 (May 2011), at http://www.domusweb.it/en/interview/the-life-geometric/. Accessed May 20, 2013.

Personally, I am ambivalent on the issue of credit. The visual evidence is on the side of a decisive contribution by Tyng. Never before or after did Kahn make a building remotely like the City Tower. It is also true, however, that none of Tyng's independent work approaches the sophistication of the City Tower. Perhaps a compelling argument can be made for this as an ideal collaboration: two architects, coming from different places but with a strong personal chemistry, making something that neither would have been capable of on their own.

Fuller himself claims credit for the geometry of the ceiling of the Yale Art Gallery, suggesting that he "converted" Kahn to geodesic thinking on their train rides to New Haven. See K. Michael Hays, "Fuller's Geological Engagements with Architecture," in Buckminster Fuller: Starting with the Universe, ed. K. Michael Hays and Dana Miller (New Haven: Yale University Press and the Whitney Museum of American Art, 2008), 19; and Irene E. Ayad, "Louis Kahn and Space Frames," Beyond the Cube, The Architecture of Space Frames and Polyhedra (New York: Wiley & Sons, 1997), 229. Those who have looked carefully at the chronology suggest that this would have been impossible, as the geometry was in place before Kahn started commuting to Yale. See Goldhagen, Louis Kahn's Situated Modernism, 65. Tyng recalls Kahn pushing pencils through the voids of her Bucks County Schoolhouse project to test how the

mechanical ducts might be threaded through the depth of the tetrahedral geometry. Here, too, the evidence points to Tyng's contribution, but the realization in concrete renders it closer to Kahn's sensibility.

In any event, it is clear that Fuller tended to be proprietary about his discoveries. The sculptor Kenneth Snelson, who studied with Fuller at Black Mountain College, wrote, "I believed, literally, because he claimed so, that before Buckminster Fuller came along, no human had ever noticed, for example, that to inscribe the diagonals of the square faces of a cube was to define two interlocking tetrahedra within. Students joked that, after all, hadn't Bucky invented the triangle? None of us knew, for example, of Alexander Graham Bell's early space frames, nor anything at all about crystallography." Tensegrity wiki, at http://tensegrity.wikispaces.com/Snelson%2C+Kenneth. Accessed May 20, 2013.

8. Philip Johnson, quoted in Hays, "Fuller's Geological Engagements with Architecture," 2 .

9. This is a complicated issue and beyond the scope of this essay. Briefly, I would say that although it is hard to reconcile Kahn's tectonics of mass with Venturi's paper-thin facades—and Kahn resisted the idea that architecture could ever be reduced to a sign system—Kahn's elementalism is a necessary precondition of Venturi's architecture of signs and symbols. Before you can think of architecture as available linguistic material (words and phrases that can be combined and recombined), you have to break it down into its constituent parts. That is exactly what Kahn did, which in turn gave Venturi a series of ready-made elements to freely manipulate, divorced from their original tectonic character.

STAN ALLEN

Stan Allen is an architect and George Dutton '27 Professor of Architectural Design at the Princeton University School of Architecture, where he served as dean from 2002 to 2012. His practice, SAA/Stan Allen Architect, has realized buildings and projects from single-family houses to urban master plans, in the United States and abroad. The extensive catalog of architectural and urban strategies he developed to respond to the complexity of the modern city is presented in Points and Lines: Diagrams and Projects for the City (1999), and his essays are collected in Practice: Architecture, Technique and Representation (2009). His most recent book is Landform Building: Architecture's New Terrain (2011).

DANIEL LÓPEZ-PÉREZ

Daniel López-Pérez, a Ph.D. candidate at the Princeton University School of Architecture, is an assistant professor of architectural design and founding faculty member of the architecture program at the University of San Diego. In 2009 he coedited The Function of Form, a comparative taxonomy of structural and formal systems. A Fuller scholar, López-Pérez is currently completing the manuscript of a book entitled R. Buckminster Fuller's Spherical Atlas, 1944–1980.

ALEJANDRO ZAERA-POLO

Alejandro Zaera-Polo is dean of the Princeton University School of Architecture. The internationally renowned architect and scholar previously served as dean of the Berlage Institute in Rotterdam, occupied the Berlage Chair at the Delft University of Technology in the Netherlands, and held the Norman R. Foster Visiting Professorship of Architectural Design at Yale University. Widely published in leading journals, such as El Croquis, Quaderns, and A+U, his essays are collected in The Sniper's Log: An Architectural Perspective of Generation-X (2012). The award-winning work of Zaera-Polo's firm, AZPA, includes the Yokohama International Cruise Terminal in Japan, distinguished by its dramatic form and innovative use of materials.

Published by
Princeton Architectural Press
37 East Seventh Street
New York, New York 10003

Visit our website at www.papress.com.

© 2014 Princeton University School of Architecture
All rights reserved
Printed and bound in China
17 16 15 14   4 3 2 1 First edition

No part of this book may be used or reproduced in any manner without written
permission from the publisher, except in the context of reviews.

The editors would like to acknowledge the Barr Ferree Foundation Fund, Department of
Art and Archaeology, Princeton University, and the Faculty Research Fund, University
of San Diego, for their generous support of this publication.

R. Buckminster Fuller's images courtesy the Estate of R. Buckminster Fuller. Fuller's
words from his previously unpublished 1966 Kassler lecture and from the Synergetics
Dictionary: The Mind of Buckminster Fuller, compiled and edited by E. J. Applewhite
© The Estate of R. Buckminster Fuller. All rights reserved.

Every reasonable attempt has been made to identify owners of copyright.
Errors or omissions will be corrected in subsequent editions.

The Kassler Lectures Series Editor: Stan Allen
Managing Editor, SoA Books: Nancy Eklund Later
Project Editor, Princeton Architectural Press: Megan Carey
Design: Omnivore

Library of Congress Cataloging-in-Publication Data
   R. Buckminster Fuller : world man / Daniel López-Pérez, editor, with contributions by
Alejandro Zaera-Polo and Stan Allen. — First [edition].
      pages cm. — (The Kassler Lectures)
   Includes bibliographical references.
   ISBN 978-1-61689-094-0 (pbk.)
1. Architecture and globalization. 2. Architecture—Environmental aspects. 3.
Architecture—Economic aspects. 4. Fuller, R. Buckminster (Richard Buckminster),
1895–1983—Criticism and interpretation. I. López, Daniel (López-Pérez), editor of
compilation. II. Fuller, R. Buckminster (Richard Buckminster), 1895–1983. World man.
III. Title. IV. Title: World man.
   NA2543.G46R2 2013
   720.1'03—dc23
                              2013024619